I0074549

THE
FISHPOND
ADVANTAGE

Break Free, Build Systems, and Live on Your Terms

AMOS MAKUMBE

Copyright

Copyright © 2025 by Amos Makumbe

All rights reserved.

No part of this publication may be reproduced, distributed, or transmitted in any form or by any means, including photocopying, recording, or other electronic or mechanical methods, without the prior written permission of the publisher, except as permitted by US copyright law.

ISBN: 978-1-83492-268-3

Table of Contents

Introduction 7

A New Perspective on Success 11

Breaking the Academic Illusion..................................... 27

Creativity The Seed of Innovation.................................. 39

The Power of Practical Learning 59

The Corporate Ladder Trap 71

The System of Independence... 85

Facing the Storms 105

Sharing the Harvest.. 137

Building a Legacy of Abundance 149

Metaphor Glossary... 159

References 165

Take a deep breath,

let go of the anchor,

and prepare to set sail into uncharted waters.

Introduction

Leaving the Shore of Convention

Imagine standing on the shore, where the land feels safe and familiar, gazing at the vast ocean. The waves lap at your feet, inviting you to explore the horizon, but the voices around you urge caution. They remind you that there is only one safe way to navigate life, which is a straight and narrow route marked by academic credentials and corporate hierarchies—a prescribed path others have charted before you.

It's the world of suits and briefcases, where smiles are tight, conversations revolve around quarterly goals, and those who fall in line climb steadily up the ladder. The rebels and dreamers are politely and quietly dismissed. But what if that shore isn't the only place you're meant to be? Staying close to the coast may feel secure, but it limits your view of the possibilities beyond.

This book is your invitation to step off the shore and let the cold water awaken you to challenge the idea that the only way to success is through the narrow channels of tradition.

Consider questioning whether the system you've been taught to trust is right for you and recognize its limitations; then, decide if it truly aligns with your unique talents and vision of life.

Set Sail on Your Own Terms

This is not a book of rigid rules or step-by-step instructions. It's a collection of perspectives, metaphors, stories, tales, and tools to help you design a life that's authentically yours. As you set sail, remember that the journey isn't about reaching one final destination but about discovering the countless possibilities that unfold when you finally take control of your destiny.

This is James Bond's World

Picture yourself stepping into the uncharted waters where the familiar no longer applies and you're forced to rely on your instincts. This reminds me of an unforgettable moment from the 2002 James Bond movie Die Another Day, starring Pierce Brosnan as James Bond.

In the movie, Bond is "handed the keys" to a custom-designed Aston Martin V12 Vanquish, also known as the "invisible car," an engineering marvel equipped with state-of-the-art gadgets, including missile launchers, target-seeking short-range guns, an ejector seat, and adaptive camouflage.

Alongside this high-tech masterpiece, Bond is also given a thick manual detailing the car's features and functionalities. In true Bond style, however, he doesn't even open the manual. Instead, he uses the car's weaponry to obliterate the manual in a spectacular show of confidence and irreverence. Without hesitation, he gets behind the wheel and drives off, ready to figure out its capabilities in real time.

- **Confidence in Your Abilities**

  Bond's casual destruction of the manual reflects supreme confidence in his resourcefulness. Where most people might pause in fearing the unknown or doubting their capabilities, Bond demonstrated a willingness to trust himself. He understood that he had the tools, instincts, and adaptability to handle whatever came his way.

  In life, this kind of confidence can be transformative. Too often, we second-guess ourselves or wait until we feel "fully prepared." Bond's approach reminds us that sometimes, we already have what it takes to succeed. By choosing action over preparation, Bond shows the power of learning by doing. Instead of getting bogged down in theoretical knowledge or overthinking every detail, he dives in. Action creates momentum, and mistakes become valuable lessons.

Think of the first day you stepped into the office, starting your first job. Your palms were sweaty as you shook hands with your new colleagues, and in meetings, every unfamiliar buzzword felt like a foreign language. Your voice trembled, and your slides were out of order during your first presentation. But you got through it. With each new challenge, your confidence grows. One day, without even realizing it, you became the person helping new employees navigate their first awkward moments. Hands-on experience often teaches us what no amount of preparation can.

- **Breaking the Rules**

Bond challenges the idea that rules and conventions are sacred. Instead of blindly adhering to the guidelines, he trusts his judgment and creativity to navigate the situation.

What about you? Think about the rules you've been taught to follow in your own life regarding career, relationships, or personal goals. Think about a time when you hesitated to follow your passion because it didn't fit the safe career path you were taught to pursue. What might have happened if you had the guts to follow your instincts instead of the rules? What opportunities might you have missed?

Sometimes, breaking away from convention is the only way to unlock your true potential. Life rarely comes with a clear set of instructions.

Be the Driver, Not the Reader

- o Are you ready to stop following someone else's rules?
- o Are you ready to trust your instincts rather than depend excessively on external guidance?
- o Are you ready to discard the manual and navigate the unknown with confidence?

Embrace uncertainty, break free from conventions, and trust in your abilities. Take the wheel and drive boldly into the future.

Success is not the key to happiness. Happiness is the key to success. If you love what you are doing, you will be successful

Albert Schweitzer

Chapter 1

A New Perspective on Success

Imagine unfolding a crinkled, centuries-old paper map with smudged and torn edges. You look around, trying to make sense of it, but the landmarks no longer exist. The city's streets no longer match the lines on the page. A highway is cutting through what was once a quiet square, and skyscrapers rise where blank spaces were. Frustrated, you wander, realizing that this map handed down by society is useless in this modern city.

This antiquated societal map prescribes a well-trodden path: study hard, earn degrees, secure a stable job, and climb the corporate ladder. Each rung climbed is a promise of financial stability and social approval, but for many of us, this promise has become elusive. We've worked hard, we've followed the prescribed steps, and we've climbed the ladder, only to find ourselves stuck in a cycle of paycheck-to-paycheck survival, wondering if we'll ever feel the fulfillment we were promised.

What if the map itself is the problem because it's outdated and incapable of guiding us through today's dynamic world?

When the map no longer serves us, we need something better. Something that reflects the ever-changing nature of our lives and helps us navigate with clarity and purpose. We need a tool that adapts to us, and this tool is a compass that guides us based on our values, passions, and purpose.

Unlike a map, a compass doesn't prescribe a single route. It won't tell you to follow the road paved by someone else or aim for destinations chosen by others. Instead, a compass points you to your true north, which contains your passions, values, dreams, and long-term goals. It encourages self-discovery, guiding you to align your actions with what truly matters to you.

In our modern world, success is no longer about following someone else's directions. It's about charting your course, following a compass. Trusting your compass might mean leaving a traditional corporate job to pursue a passion, starting a business that aligns with your values, or simply redefining success on your terms. You stop following preordained routes and begin to become the creator of your journey.

Choosing the compass means you step into a mindset that values curiosity over conformity, exploration over predictability, and purpose over societal approval. It's time to set aside the old map and navigate the future with freedom, creativity, and individuality, holding a compass in your hand.

The Compass Mindset

At graduations, families beam with pride as their children toss their caps of knowledge into the air in celebration. Degrees are handed out like trophies, symbols of hard work, intellect, and societal approval. They're celebrated as milestones, from family gatherings to corporate boardrooms, but are we celebrating thinkers, creators, and problem solvers, or merely those equipped to maintain systems built by others?

This is not a critique of education itself. Education is a powerful tool, an essential foundation for growth and empowerment. However, it is incomplete if it does not inspire creativity, independence, or empower individuals to make a meaningful impact. Think of students who graduated at the top of their class, only to feel lost in the 'real world,' unsure of how to apply their knowledge to make a meaningful impact. A degree is not the finish line but a stepping stone.

Let's face it: we need to complement traditional education by offering a different perspective, one that emphasizes entrepreneurship, creativity, and the pursuit of independence. Understanding the roots of our education system and challenging its limitations can unlock the potential to forge paths that align with our passions and create legacies for generations to come.

The compass mindset is about rethinking success, not as a predetermined destination set by society, but as a journey you design for yourself.

Earl Nightingale once said, "A success is anyone who is doing deliberately a predetermined job, because that's what he decided to do deliberately."

> Who succeeds? The only person who succeeds is the person who is progressively realizing a worthy idea. It is the person who said, 'I am going to become this,' and then began to work towards that goal. I will tell you who the successful people are: success is the schoolteacher who is teaching at a school because that's what he or she wants to do; success is the woman who is a wife and mother because she wanted to become a wife and mother and is doing a good job of it; success is a man running a corner gas station because that was his dream and that's what he wanted to do; success is a successful salesman and wants to become a top-notch salesman and grow and build his organization; success is anyone who is doing deliberately a predetermined job because that's what he decided to do deliberately. [1]

Your compass empowers you to navigate uncharted territories and build a life that reflects your unique values, passions, and goals. Most of us are conditioned early to associate success with the traditional milestones mentioned earlier. Of course, these accomplishments have value, but they are not the sole measure of a fulfilling life.

---

1.   Earl Nightingale, How to Completely Change Your Life in 30 Seconds.

History is filled with individuals who defied these conventional paths to achieve extraordinary impact. Take Sir Richard Branson, the founder of the Virgin Group and a globally renowned entrepreneur. Struggling with dyslexia and poor academic performance, Branson dropped out of school at 16 to pursue his passions. He defied societal norms and built an empire comprising more than 400 companies across various sectors, including music, airlines, and space tourism. Sir Richard Branson was knighted in the year 2000 for his "services to entrepreneurship."

> Richard Branson, founder of the Virgin Group, quit school at 16 to start a magazine, paving the way for a vast business empire that includes airlines and space tourism. Branson's adventurous spirit and innovative approach to business have earned him a substantial fortune and a knighthood.[2]

Countless others rewrote the rules and carved their paths to success. Like Richard Branson, they proved that thinking creatively, acting independently, and building systems aligned with their dreams and values are what truly set people apart. Larry Ellison is another extraordinary individual whose journey defied convention and reshaped an entire industry.

His aunt and uncle raised Ellison in a modest household in Chicago after his teenage mother gave him up for adoption. Despite these early challenges, Ellison discovered a passion for programming and engineering. He briefly attended the University of Illinois and later the University of Chicago but traditional education didn't resonate with him, and he dropped out of both schools. Many might have seen this as a setback, but for Ellison, it was a turning point.

---

2.   10 School Dropouts Who Became Billionaires, https://businesselitesafrica.com/10-school-dropouts-who-became-billionaires/?v=a1555463c361

Fueled by his curiosity and determination, he taught himself the necessary skills. He followed his compass toward a bold vision, one that would eventually lead him to co-found Oracle Corporation, one of the world's largest and most influential software companies. His work not only revolutionized the software industry but also demonstrated how thinking differently and staying true to your passions can lead to extraordinary outcomes.

Ellison's journey illustrates the power of aligning success with passion. He didn't let his lack of a degree or humble beginnings define his potential. Instead, he stayed aligned with his passion for programming and used his creativity and determination to build something extraordinary.

> Larry Ellison, another prominent dropout, left college twice and was once told by his adoptive father that he would amount to nothing. He proved this prediction wrong by founding Oracle in 1977, a company that would grow to become the world's second-largest software maker. Today, Ellison is worth $176.6 billion and still plays a significant role in Oracle as its chairman and chief technology officer.[3]
>
> One of his memorable quotes is "The most important aspect of my personality as far as determining my success goes has been my questioning of conventional wisdom, doubting experts, and questioning authority. While that can be painful in relationships with your parents and teachers, it's enormously useful in life."[4]

The stories of individuals like Richard Branson and Larry Ellison illustrate the power of the compass mindset.

---

3.   https://businesselitesafrica.com/10-school-dropouts-who-became-billion-aires/?v=a1555463c361

4.   Your Story, https://yourstory.com/2017/01/larry-ellison-inspirational-quotes

They remind us that success isn't about passively following prescribed paths. It's about actively designing our journeys guided by our passions and values and using challenges as stepping stones to greatness.

The journey is not easy. Courage is needed to navigate uncharted waters where the waves are unpredictable and the horizon is unknown. It means facing uncertainty and risking judgment from others who cling to conventional definitions of success, but in the quest, you gain the freedom to build something uniquely your own. And in doing so, you unlock the ability to create not just a life worth living, but a legacy worth leaving.

This is more than a personal achievement. This is about building a world where others can thrive alongside you. It's about using your talents and creativity to design systems that empower communities, solve problems, and inspire change.

When you embrace the compass mindset, it's like stepping off a crowded highway filled with rush-hour traffic onto an open, tranquil trail winding through the wilderness. The familiar signs and rules disappear, and for the first time, you hold the power to choose your direction.

The journey is yours to define. The compass is in your hands. Feel the crunch of leaves underfoot and the fresh air filling your lungs. Are you ready to take the first step toward a life that's authentically yours?

The Treadmill of Achievement

Have you ever felt as if success is a treadmill you can't get off? You work harder and faster, expecting to arrive somewhere meaningful, only to realize you're stuck in one place. The steady hum of the treadmill and the pounding of your feet echoing in your mind is not progress you're hearing, but it's exhaustion. You are being drained and disillusioned.

This treadmill exists because society's definition of success is focused almost entirely on external achievements, leaving little room to consider the deeper, internal aspects of fulfillment. To understand this dynamic, it's essential to distinguish between two types of success:

- **External Success:** These are the tangible rewards, such as wealth, titles, and social recognition. They're easy to measure and often celebrated by society, making them the default benchmark for achievement. External success can provide comfort and validation, but it usually fails to satisfy the more profound yearning for meaning and purpose.

- **Internal Success:** This is the intangible sense of fulfillment that comes from living in alignment with your values, passions, and vision. It's about contributing to the world in a way that resonates with your true self. Unlike external success, internal success cannot be measured by societal standards because it's deeply personal. Internal success might mean pursuing a creative passion, building meaningful relationships, or using your talents to make a positive impact in your community.

External success often clashes with the more profound desire for internal fulfillment, leaving many torn between societal expectations and their true selves.

Malala Yousafzai's life is a powerful example of internal success triumphing over external pressures. Growing up in Pakistan, she faced immense danger simply for advocating for girls' education. At the age of 15, she was targeted and nearly killed by the Taliban for her activism. Yet, instead of retreating into fear or pursuing material safety, Malala redoubled her efforts on her mission.

Her compass pointed her toward a path of global advocacy, driven by an unwavering belief in the power of education. Despite nearly losing her life, she refused to let fear silence her voice. Instead, she turned her pain into purpose, fighting for the rights of millions of girls to learn and thrive.

By the age of 17, she became the youngest recipient of the Nobel Peace Prize, not for seeking recognition but because her impact demanded it. Malala's success isn't defined by her fame or accolades; it's measured by the millions of girls who now have access to education because of her tireless efforts.

Malala's story shows the transformative power of living with purpose, guided by internal values rather than external pressures. In contrast, adhering to predefined paths, such as rigid career tracks, chasing titles, or prioritizing financial success above all else, encourages competition rather than fostering creation.

The irony is that no matter how hard you run, the treadmill doesn't take you closer to personal fulfillment. It merely keeps you moving, often at the expense of your well-being, creativity, and independence. True success isn't universal; it's personal. It's not about running harder toward external milestones but about stepping off the treadmill and creating a life that reflects your deepest aspirations and values. Do you dream of building a life where your days are fueled by purpose and joy, living authentically with your passions and purpose?

Rethink Your Path

Many of us follow a life script written by our families, passed down from one generation to the next. Family traditions play a critical role in shaping us. Sticking to this script may bring family satisfaction, but it often leads to frustration, stagnation, and the painful realization that you're living someone else's life.

What if you could write your script for your life? It's time to stop following the lines written for you by others and take control of the story.

Your life is like a blank page. No one can write it for you. The ink isn't set yet. This time, you decide what happens next. Pick a pen, and stand before the blank page filled with possibilities. As you begin to write your story, what lead role would you take as the main character? Consider these questions as you begin to rewrite your script:

- Would you prioritize financial stability, or would you take risks to pursue a passion?
- Would you stay in the safety of familiar roads or venture into uncharted territories to create something new?
- Would you keep following the crowd or carve out a unique path that reflects your individuality?

Rewriting your script is an exciting opportunity, but where do you start? Like any great story, your journey needs a strong foundation, a clear direction, and intentional choices. Here are the steps to help you take control of your narrative and begin designing a life that's truly your own:

i.   Reflect on Your Current Path:

Are you living according to your values, or are you stuck on a road dictated by external expectations? What truly brings you joy and fulfillment, and what are you compromising for the sake of others' approval? Reflecting on your current path is the first step to aligning your life with your true north. Take stock of what truly fulfills you and identify areas where you're out of alignment.

A lawyer, burdened by the daily grind of his legal career, might find himself longing for something more meaningful.

Reflecting on his path, he may discover that his true passion lies in storytelling and writing novels, which he had ignored for years. Stepping back and reevaluating his priorities can be the catalyst for taking the first steps toward a career that aligns with his creative aspirations.

Similarly, Sonia's journey demonstrates how reflecting on your current path can lead to a complete transformation and uncover a new passion. Sonia, a doctor by profession, chose to set aside the title of 'Dr.' to follow her true calling. Her passion for fashion and beauty inspired her to leave the medical field behind and carve a new path as a blogger.

Through her platform, Sheer Vanity by Sonia, she celebrates style and aesthetics while sharing her unique vision with the world. Soon, she plans to expand her journey further by venturing into fashion design, proving that embracing your passions can lead to an entirely new chapter in life.

> "Being a doctor is considered a noble profession, but my heart was never in it. I never felt like it was my calling; I was only Dr. Sonia because my parents were hell-bent on it. I'm almost the black sheep of my family because I'm literally the only non-doctor in my house now.
>
> I'm not a person who opens up easily, but when you ask me about fashion, I can talk a mile a minute. Being a blogger has changed me as a person; I am now more open and can talk to even more people because I truly love what I do.
>
> The eyebrows you see on my face are literally tattooed on; I have none. When I was 12, I started filling in my eyebrows because I was pretty insecure about how I looked. That's where my love for beauty grew in leaps & bounds. I worked on this, entered contests & practiced watching YouTube tutorials. I started with this & then posted my first YouTube makeup look.
>
> Every morning I wake up & thank the universe for allowing me to push myself into this field. Every day is a new day— of course it has its ups and downs, but I'm very content, & I'm learning new things about life each day." [5]

---

5. Stories Of 9 Indians, https://homegrown.co.in/homegrown-voices/stories-of-10-indians-who-quit-stable-jobs-to-pursue-their-passions.

ii. Define Your Vision:

Once you've reflected on your current path, the next step is to imagine where you truly want to go. Close your eyes and picture what success looks like to you.

How would you like to feel waking up each morning? Let yourself dream boldly and authentically. Then, write down your aspirations, both big and small.

Create a vision that feels exciting and authentic. This vision will become your compass, guiding you toward a life aligned with your passions and purpose. Take the example of a teacher. Inspired by her love for education and the struggles her students faced outside the classroom, she might envision creating a community center.

She imagines students walking through its doors to find mentorship programs, academic support, and a safe space where they feel truly seen and empowered. This vision is the first step in transforming her passion into reality.

Your vision doesn't need to be perfect or even fully formed. Let it reflect what excites you, what inspires you, and what feels authentic to who you are. Writing your aspirations down is powerful. It brings clarity, focus, and momentum. It transforms your ideas from abstract thoughts into tangible goals you can work toward.

iii. Experiment and Explore:

Success isn't a straight line from X to Y but a winding journey of discovery full of twists, turns, and surprises. It's about the excitement of trying something new, the resilience to embrace failure, the courage to adapt, and the joy of finding unexpected opportunities along the way.

Experimenting and exploring new paths helps you uncover passions and possibilities you might otherwise never have considered. Start small, whether it's launching a side project, learning a new skill, or connecting with mentors who inspire you.

Taking small steps helps minimize risk while allowing you to explore your interests, build confidence, and gain clarity about what truly excites you.

Take the story of a corporate employee with a passion for baking. After years of working in an office, she began experimenting on weekends, selling her homemade treats at a local market.

Each sale fuels her confidence, and each smile from a happy customer reminds her why she started. Or think of someone who loves fitness but feels trapped in a desk job. On weekends, he begins teaching yoga classes at a community center, feeling a spark of fulfillment he hasn't felt in years.

Then there's the aspiring writer who starts a blog, nervously hitting 'publish' on his first post, only to find joy in the act of sharing his story by seeing the likes and comments from his new community. These small steps allow you to test the waters and discover paths that could lead to new, fulfilling opportunities.

Remember, failure isn't a setback, but it's feedback. Every misstep teaches you something valuable and brings you closer to discovering what truly works for you. The more you experiment, the more you learn about yourself and the possibilities that align with your true north.

iv. Build Your System:

Passion alone can spark the fire, but it takes sustainable systems to keep it burning. These systems are the unseen scaffolding that supports your journey, like creating financial stability, building a network of supportive people, and developing habits that nurture your personal and professional growth.

Visualize these systems as the solid foundation of a house, giving you the stability to focus on what you love without constantly worrying about it all falling apart. With strong systems in place, you then gain the freedom to grow, adapt, and pursue your passions with confidence.

For example, consider a tech enthusiast who spends his weekends working on freelance coding projects. With each completed project, his confidence grows, and he begins to see the possibility of transitioning into a full-time career in software development.

These small, deliberate steps create a system that allows his passions to flourish without unnecessary risk. You don't need to have every piece of the puzzle figured out from the start.

You need to begin. Maybe it's setting aside a few hours a week to develop a side project, creating a budget to manage your income streams, or reaching out to a mentor who can guide you. Build and let your system evolve.

v. Stay Resilient:

The road less traveled is rarely smooth. Challenges and detours are inevitable, and it's natural to feel fear or self-doubt along the way. You might wonder if you're on the right path or if you should turn back, but these moments are also opportunities to grow stronger, to learn, and to prove to yourself that you can navigate even the toughest terrain.

Every challenge you face and overcome sharpens your skills and strengthens your resolve. Here is the story of a comedian who dreams of building his comic show while juggling a full-time job.

Initially, rejection emails accumulate, and a smaller audience than expected attends his first show. The applause is polite, but not the uproarious laughter he envisioned. It's disheartening, but he keeps going, rewriting jokes, perfecting his delivery, refining his craft, and learning what works. Slowly, the momentum builds with more laughter, more viewers, and eventually, a thriving business that reflects his vision and passion. Staying with what he loves turns early setbacks into stepping stones for his success.

Rowan Atkinson, known as Mr. Bean, struggled with a stutter and an unconventional comedic style that initially wasn't widely appreciated. His unique approach to visual and physical humor didn't always resonate well in the early years of his career, making it challenging for him to gain recognition in the mainstream entertainment industry.

Atkinson's breakthrough came when producers of the BBC show "Not the Nine O'Clock News" recognized his talent and gave him a chance to be part of the cast. This program became a hit, establishing Atkinson as a household name in the UK.

His success in "Not the Nine O'Clock News" led to his role in "Blackadder" and later the globally renowned series "Mr. Bean," both of which leveraged his unique style of humor and achieved international success by his thirties.

Atkinson has often spoken about the importance of authenticity and perseverance in his work. He emphasized that success comes from staying true to yourself and your vision, regardless of external criticism.

An inspiring quote from him is, "The people who succeed are irrationally passionate about something." [6]

Always remember that the roads you choose today shape the terrain you'll traverse tomorrow. Dare to take one small step today toward the journey only you can define.

The Story of Gillian Lynne

Gillian Lynne's story is a powerful example of what happens when people align their lives with their true north. As a child, she struggled in school, unable to conform to the traditional educational standards. She was constantly fidgeting, unable to sit still, and her teachers believed she had a learning disorder. Her school wrote to her parents, suggesting that something might be wrong with her.

---

6.   The Ideal Mindset, https://www.youtube.com/watch?v=eHGL-me0Baw

Her mother, concerned, took Gillian to a specialist. As she described the issues, the doctor listened and observed Gillian. Then he said to her mother, "Let's step outside for a moment." As they left the room, the doctor turned on the radio. From the hallway, they watched as Gillian instantly got up and started moving to the music. The doctor turned to her mother and said something life-changing: "Mrs. Lynne, Gillian isn't sick. She's a dancer. Take her to a dance school."

Her mother followed this advice, and Gillian was introduced to a world where she met people like herself, individuals who needed to move to think and express themselves. She thrived in that environment and eventually became one of the most successful choreographers in history, creating iconic musicals such as Cats and The Phantom of the Opera.

Sir Ken Robinson used this story in his TED talk, "Do Schools Kill Creativity?" to illustrate the broader point that many children who struggle in traditional education systems are not "broken" or "failing."

Instead, they may be in the wrong environment, one that doesn't recognize or nurture their natural abilities. He emphasized that education systems should focus on discovering and developing everyone's unique talents rather than forcing everyone to conform to a single standard.

Gillian's story reminds us that success is not a one-size-fits-all recipe, but it is as diverse as the talents, passions, and values that define us. Her journey shows that embracing what makes you different can be the key to achieving extraordinary things. What others saw as a problem was Gillian Lynne's greatest strength, waiting to be nurtured. With the proper support, she turned what made her different into an extraordinary gift, culminating in her becoming one of the most celebrated choreographers in the world. As you navigate your journey, remember to embrace what makes you different and seek environments that nurture your talents. The path may not always be smooth, but it will always be worth it.

What once worked for factory floors doesn't work for innovation-driven economies.

Chapter 2

Breaking the Academic Illusion

At the dawn of the industrial age, humanity faced a profound transformation. Agrarian economies, where knowledge and skills were passed down through families and small communities, were giving way to the mechanized power of industrial systems. The sound of machines whirring and assembly lines clattering marked the rise of centralized production. For the first time, societies faced a pressing challenge: how to train vast numbers of workers quickly and uniformly to meet the growing demands of factory-based economies.

Public education emerged as the solution. It was designed to mold disciplined, literate, and punctual individuals who could efficiently operate within a highly structured system. The classroom mirrored the factory floor, with its rigid schedules, standardized tasks, and hierarchical authority. Students, like workers, were conditioned to follow instructions, complete tasks on time, adhere to routines, and adapt to repetitive processes with precision. The bell signaled shifts in lessons, just as whistles signaled shifts on the production line.

This system was revolutionary for its time, democratizing access to basic education and lifting entire societies out of illiteracy and ignorance. It provided the intellectual foundation necessary for industrialization, fueling innovation and creating a workforce capable of sustaining the economic engine of the Industrial Revolution. Public education played a pivotal role in shaping modern economies, offering pathways out of poverty for many and driving unprecedented societal progress. But the world has changed dramatically since then. While machines once drove human progress, today's world demands something entirely different: creativity, critical thinking, and adaptability. The skills required to thrive in today's interconnected, innovation-driven world bear little resemblance to those needed on the factory floor. Yet, despite this seismic shift, our education system remains stuck in the past.

Think of a high school senior sitting at her desk, staring at the clock as the teacher lectures about formulas she'll need to memorize for an exam. Despite being intelligent and curious, she feels stifled, disconnected, and unsure how any of this prepares her for the future she dreams of. She wants to create, innovate, and build something meaningful, but instead, she's stuck learning how to pass tests and earn good grades. This is the experience of millions of students worldwide, bright individuals confined by an outdated system that was designed for a world that no longer exists. This disconnect perpetuates what is called the academic illusion—the mistaken belief that traditional education alone is sufficient to prepare individuals for modern success. The factory-model classroom trains students to conform and complete repetitive tasks, but it does little to cultivate the creativity and adaptability they need to navigate an increasingly unpredictable future.

The question we must then ask ourselves is, how can we break free from this outdated system and reimagine education for the modern world?

Rapid technological advancements, globalization, and the emergence of artificial intelligence are defining characteristics of the 21st century. These forces have created a dynamic, interconnected world where adaptability, problem-solving, and innovation are no longer optional but essential.

Workers no longer thrive by simply following instructions; they succeed by imagining solutions, thinking critically, and embracing constant change. Breaking free from the academic illusion means recognizing the limitations of traditional education and daring to explore new possibilities. The world no longer needs obedient factory workers but rather innovators, thinkers, and creators.

A Legacy That No Longer Fits

We are left with a system that prioritizes conformity over creativity, memorization over problem-solving, and standardization over individuality. In an era where technology can perform repetitive tasks and process vast amounts of information, the real value lies in human ingenuity: the ability to think critically, adapt to change, and envision solutions for complex challenges.

Many students, brimming with unique talents and ideas, find themselves stifled in classrooms that reward compliance over originality. A gifted artist sits in frustration, sketching in the margins of his notebook while the lesson demands rote memorization. A natural problem-solver grows disengaged; their curiosity dulled by lessons that prioritize textbook answers over exploring real-world challenges.

The industrial roots of education, while once groundbreaking, now risk holding us back. Instead of preparing students for a world of opportunity, it locks them into a framework that no longer aligns with the demands of our modern society.

The Monoculture of Ideas

Imagine a vast, uniform field, each seed planted in perfect rows with the expectation that every plant will grow into the same type of tree. The soil is carefully tilled, not to cultivate a variety of crops but to ensure uniformity. Wildflowers are uprooted, and unique crops are unwelcome.

This monoculture approach might appear efficient, yielding a consistent crop. But over time, its flaws become apparent. Without diversity, the soil becomes depleted. The field grows vulnerable to pests, diseases, and changing conditions. This monoculture of ideas mirrors our education system. Although it may have been efficient in the past, it ultimately limited growth and innovation. To thrive in today's world, we must embrace diversity in education, nurture unique talents, encourage divergent thinking, and create environments that nurture students' individual growth and development.

A System That Rewards Conformity

Look back at your own time in school. What were you rewarded for? For generations, compliance has been the ultimate value in education. Students were rewarded not for original thinking or bold ideas but for their ability to absorb the "correct" information and regurgitate it in the right way. Creative problem-solving and curiosity are often discouraged rather than nurtured. Those who ask big questions, think outside the box, or possess unconventional talents are usually labeled as disruptive or underachieving, with their potential left untapped. In this system, success belongs to those who learn to fit in. The students who memorize answers, follow instructions, and perform in ways that align with the system's narrow expectations are the ones who are rewarded with high grades, degrees, and access to prestigious opportunities.

Today, we face challenges that require creative solutions. We have problems that can't be solved by simply following instructions. The need for dynamic thinkers—individuals who can adapt, experiment, and create—has never been greater. Yet the education system, in many ways, still clings to its monocultural roots, prioritizing uniformity over diversity of thought.

The Need for Diverse Seeds of Thought

Just imagine an educational ecosystem where every student is seen as a unique seed, planted in fertile soil that nourishes their individuality. In this system, not every seed is expected to grow into the same kind of tree. Some might rise as towering oaks, their branches stretching toward the sky, while others bloom as wildflowers, small but vibrant, spreading beauty wherever they grow. Still others might creep like vines, connecting and supporting the ecosystem as they intertwine with one another.

This is the power of diversity in education. It creates an environment where students are free to grow in their direction. One student might sprout into an innovative entrepreneur, challenging the limits of technology. Another might flourish as an artist, expressing truths through their creativity. Yet another might find their roots as an activist, championing justice and equity, while others grow into engineers, scientists, or caregivers who enrich the world in countless ways. Such a system wouldn't just prepare students to memorize and replicate knowledge but would encourage them to challenge assumptions, question norms, and develop creative solutions to real-world problems. It would value experimentation, curiosity, and the exploration of new ideas, recognizing that progress doesn't come from sameness but from the synergy of different perspectives and talents.

To build this world, we must start by planting the seeds of creativity, curiosity, and individuality in every classroom—a classroom where students aren't judged by how well they fit into a mold, but by how boldly they pursue their passions. Teachers then act as gardeners, tending to each student's growth, helping them thrive in their way. This is the future education we need, one that celebrates the diversity of thought.

The Finnish Education Approach

This vision of a garden of ideas isn't just wishful thinking, as it has already been implemented in some parts of the world, where students are encouraged to think critically, collaborate with peers, and explore their passions without the pressure of constant testing. In Finland, this is the reality. Their education system has redefined what success looks like by focusing on individuality, well-being, and the 4Cs: communication, collaboration, critical thinking, and creativity, rather than rote memorization and rigid standardization.

> Finland's educational reform emphasizes the skills children will need in a more digital, more integrated, and fast-paced world. These are known as the 4Cs: communication, collaboration, critical thinking, and creativity.

Another key idea in the reform is individualized instruction, which lets children learn at their own pace.

The ideas behind the reform are pushing educators to design more open and more flexible school buildings.[7]

Finland's educational philosophy represents a deliberate shift away from the traditional, test-centric approach that dominates many countries. Instead of reducing education to a race for high scores and/or intense academic competition, Finland embraces holistic learning, collaboration, and critical thinking. In Finnish classrooms, the focus is not on drilling facts for standardized tests but on nurturing curiosity, creativity, and a love of learning. The goal is to develop well-rounded individuals who are not only academically capable but also ready to make meaningful contributions to society.

Remarkably, Finnish students spend less time on homework and testing than their peers in many other nations, yet they consistently outperform them academically. Walk into a Finnish classroom, and you'll find students actively engaged in group projects, discussing ideas, or solving real-world problems. Learning feels purposeful and connected to life. It's no wonder that Finnish students also report higher levels of happiness and engagement, proving that academic success and well-being can go hand in hand.

This transformation began with a simple yet profound question: What is the purpose of education? Finland's leaders understood that the goal wasn't merely to produce students who could pass exams but to develop well-rounded individuals equipped to thrive in a rapidly changing world. They reimagined their education system with a focus on depth over breadth, understanding over rote memorization, and collaboration over competition.

---

7. Janel Siemplenski Lefort, "How the Finns do it", 21 December 2023.

Prioritizing Learning Over Testing

In many countries, standardized testing serves as the cornerstone of education, turning classrooms into 'pressure cookers' of memorization and performance. Finland, however, has taken a different approach. High-stakes exams are nearly non-existent. Instead, Finnish teachers assess students using diverse methods aligned with curriculum objectives, such as project-based work, collaborative tasks, and ongoing observation. This flexibility allows educators to focus on personalized learning, tailoring their teaching methods to suit the unique needs and interests of each student.

The only national-level assessment, the matriculation examination, occurs at the end of high school. This single exam determines eligibility for advanced studies, but by that point, students have already been evaluated holistically throughout their education. A relentless series of standardized tests does not define them; rather, it is a rich and well-rounded learning journey.

Empowered Teachers as Educational Architects

At the heart of Finland's success is its trust in teachers. Finnish educators are among the most highly trained professionals in the country, often holding master's degrees in education or specialized fields. But what truly sets them apart is the autonomy they are given. They are not restricted by rigid curricula or forced to 'teach to the test.' Instead, they are empowered to design lessons that spark curiosity, foster creativity, and adapt to their students' needs. For instance, a Finnish teacher might notice a student's passion for art and create assignments that incorporate creative projects, thus helping them to explore their interests while learning core subjects.

For another student struggling with math, the teacher might slow down and offer personalized exercises or hands-on activities to build confidence and understanding. Without the pressure of preparing students for endless exams, Finnish teachers can focus on helping each student to thrive.

This empowerment creates a culture of respect and collaboration. Teachers work closely with students to identify their strengths, address challenges, and nurture their unique talents. Classrooms are transformed into places of exploration and growth, where curiosity is encouraged and stress is minimized.

The Results Speak for Themselves

The Finnish model has consistently delivered remarkable results. Despite minimal standardized testing, Finland ranks among the top-performing countries in global education assessments, such as the Program for International Student Assessment (PISA).

Finnish students excel not because they are drilled for tests, but because they are taught to think critically, solve problems creatively, and collaborate effectively.

> Finland has been called the best country for higher education for many years. Universities in Finland are highly respected, and a degree from a Finnish university can certainly open many doors for a student. [8]

Finland's system is proof that education can be a garden of ideas, nurturing individuality, curiosity, and creativity while achieving academic excellence. While Finland's model may not be directly replicable everywhere, it offers a blueprint for other nations to rethink their priorities, reducing reliance on standardized tests, empowering teachers, and focusing on the holistic growth of students.

The question is not whether change is possible, but whether we dare to follow its lead.

---

8.   Finish Education System, https://www.edunation.co/blog/finnish-education-system-the-best-in-the-world/

The Call for a Garden of Ideas

It's time to break free from the monoculture mindset of education, one that stifles the full potential of individuals and limits the possibilities for societal progress. The future demands thinkers who can envision new ways of doing things and combine disparate ideas to solve complex problems.

Education should be a garden of ideas, where diverse seeds are nurtured to grow in ways that are true to each individual's unique potential. Only then can we truly harness the power of human creativity and innovation to meet the challenges of the modern world.

The time has come to reimagine the purpose of education. It's not a factory for producing uniform products but a fertile ground for cultivating diverse, dynamic, and creative individuals. In a world facing unprecedented challenges, we need thinkers, problem solvers, and dreamers who are ready to tackle the complexities of a rapidly changing world.

Breaking Free from the Illusion

For too long, traditional education has resembled a conveyor belt, shuttling students through a predictable sequence of stages from elementary school, high school, college, and beyond. Along the way, individuality is often sacrificed in favor of producing graduates who meet standardized criteria for conventional jobs. A degree may land you an interview, but it's your creativity, problem-solving ability, and resilience that will secure your long-term success.

Breaking free from the illusion means understanding that education is a foundation and not a ceiling. It's the starting point for exploration, not the final word on your potential. The real work begins when you step off the conveyor belt and into the world, ready to shape your path with purpose and intention. Yet, for many of us, stepping off isn't easy. Like the elephants in the story you're about to read, we are often held back by invisible ropes in the form of beliefs instilled in us by the very system we're trying to break free from.

The Elephant Rope Story

In a small village, a traveling circus became the talk of the town. Among the circus attractions were magnificent elephants, whose sheer size and power left the villagers in awe. Despite their immense strength, these elephants were tethered to the ground by nothing more than a small, flimsy rope tied around one of their legs. No chains. No cages. Just a simple rope that they could easily snap without effort. A curious villager, perplexed by the sight, approached the elephant trainer. "Why don't these elephants break free? Surely, they have the strength to do so" the villager asked.

The trainer smiled and replied, "When these elephants were very young and much smaller, we used the same type of rope to tie them. At that age, the rope was strong enough to hold them. They tried and tried to break free, but they couldn't. Over time, they learned that it was futile even to try. Now that they're fully grown, they still believe the rope is unbreakable. So, they never attempt to free themselves." The villager was stunned. These majestic creatures, capable of uprooting trees or trampling obstacles in their path, were held captive by a belief instilled in them when they were young.

The elephant rope story is a powerful metaphor for the invisible barriers we often place on ourselves. Like the elephants, we are usually tethered by limiting beliefs, which are ideas we accepted as truths in the past but that no longer hold validity in our current lives. These beliefs might stem from childhood experiences. Perhaps you've been told, "You are not good enough," or you feel societal expectations like the pressure to follow a traditional career path, or you have past failures that made you question your abilities. Some might believe that they are not qualified to start their dream business because they don't have a degree, or that it's "too late" to change careers, having already invested so much in their current path. Over time, these beliefs become invisible barriers, shaping the decisions we make and the opportunities we pursue or abandon. They dictate what we think we can or cannot achieve, often leaving us stuck in a cycle of self-doubt and fear. The irony is that many of these barriers exist only in our minds, yet they can feel as real as physical chains.

How many times have you let a false narrative hold you back? How often have you told yourself, "I can't start because..." How many dreams have you abandoned because you believed they were impossible? It's time to break free.

i. Identify Your Ropes:

Recognize the beliefs that limit you, such as fears of failure or assumptions rooted in your educational background. Write them down.

ii. Challenge the Rope:

Question these beliefs. Are they grounded in reality, or are they remnants of past experiences? Ask yourself whether they still hold true in your current life and whether they reflect the person you are today.

iii. Reframe Failure and Take Action:

View setbacks as opportunities to grow. Start by taking small steps to challenge your perceived limitations. Test the boundaries of the rope, and you'll often find it's much weaker than you thought.

iv. Seek Support and Embrace Change:

Surround yourself with people who inspire you, challenge you, and believe in your potential. Step out of your comfort zone, try new things, and explore possibilities you once dismissed.

This story is a reminder that we are often stronger and more capable than we realize. So, why is any rope still holding you back? And more importantly, are you ready to break free?

Creativity is a process of connecting disparate ideas, requiring curiosity and exposure to new experiences.

Chapter 3

Creativity The Seed of Innovation

The Compass for the Unknown

The complexities and uncertainties of real-world challenges often extend far beyond the answers found in textbooks. In these uncharted territories, creativity serves as a compass, guiding you toward new possibilities. It has the power to transform challenges into opportunities and problems into solutions, pointing the way when nothing else seems clear.

Picture yourself standing at a crossroads, surrounded by paths that stretch into the unknown. No clear signs point the way, and the choices ahead feel overwhelming. This is the reality of the modern world, where industries evolve overnight, technologies disrupt entire economies, and career paths that seemed secure yesterday might disappear tomorrow.

In moments like these, creativity becomes your most reliable tool, a compass offering direction when certainty is nowhere to be found. Just as a compass doesn't give you the entire map, creativity doesn't deliver instant answers. Instead, it helps you explore options, test ideas, and take the first step.

This is evident in the story of Hoboken's Sugarsuckle Cake Shop. When the coronavirus pandemic struck, co-founder Jen Choi faced the harsh reality of canceling their custom cake orders. The market for elaborate, bespoke cakes had disappeared overnight.

But instead of seeing this as the end, Jen treated it as a challenge. She knew families stuck at home were looking for new ways to create joy, so she pivoted. Jen launched DIY baking kits, complete with pre-measured ingredients, essential supplies, and expert tips.

These kits turned a time of fear and uncertainty into an opportunity for families to bond, experiment, and rediscover the joy of baking. What could have been a devastating blow to the business became a moment of reinvention. Creativity didn't just solve Sugarsuckle's problem but sparked new possibilities, allowing the company to adapt and even thrive during difficult times. This also shows that the essence of creativity is not just fixing what's broken but imagining what could be.

Creativity as a Skill, Not a Gift

Society often views creativity as an innate gift reserved for a select few, a mysterious talent bestowed upon artists, inventors, and visionaries. This myth stifles potential, convincing people that they're "not creative enough" to contribute meaningfully; however, the truth is that creativity isn't a mystical gift—it's a skill that anyone can develop.

Think of creativity as a muscle. Like any muscle, it grows stronger with deliberate practice and effort. Every time you step outside your comfort zone, challenge an assumption, or try something new, you're exercising this muscle. Of course, creativity comes with trial and error.

Let's say you are trying to solve a workplace issue. You might brainstorm multiple ideas, test one that seems promising, and discover that it doesn't work as you had planned; but in the process, you'll often uncover new insights or solutions you haven't considered before. Creativity isn't just for grand breakthroughs or world-changing innovations; it's also for solving everyday problems. It's for designing a product, navigating relationships, reimagining your career path, or finding joy in the mundane. Whether you're figuring out how to handle a difficult conversation or brainstorming ways to make your home more functional, creativity empowers you to see beyond limitations and imagine what it could be.

Do Schools Kill Creativity?

In his famous TED talk, 'Do Schools Kill Creativity?', Sir Ken Robinson recounts the story of a young girl in a drawing class who was deeply engrossed in her work.

> The teacher asked her, "What are you drawing?" The girl replied, "I'm drawing God." The teacher, surprised, said, "But nobody knows what God looks like." Without missing a beat, the girl responded, "They will in a minute." [8]

This profound yet straightforward anecdote captures the natural confidence and creativity of children. Unburdened by self-doubt or societal norms, they approach the world with curiosity and originality. Sir Ken Robinson uses it to emphasize how traditional education systems prioritize conformity and standardization, gradually eroding this natural sense of creativity and divergent thinking.

Robinson follows this story with another equally humorous yet insightful anecdote. He describes a nativity play in which a group of children is tasked with playing the Three Wise Men. Each child is given a line to say as they present their gift to baby Jesus.

> The first child steps forward and says, "I bring you gold." The second child follows, saying, "I bring you myrrh." The third child steps up, hesitates for a moment, and confidently says, "Frank sent this." [8]

The story is both charming and funny, capturing children's innocence and their willingness to take risks.

---

8. Do Schools Kill Creativity? https://www.ted.com/talks/sir_ken_robinson_do_schools_kill_creativity?subtitle=en.

Robinson uses it to illustrate how children are willing to make mistakes and approach things with creativity, qualities that education systems often inadvertently stifle by emphasizing correctness.

Sir Ken Robinson elaborates on the point, saying:

> "Being wrong is not the same thing as being creative. But if you're not prepared to be wrong, you'll never come up with anything original." [9]

Traditional education often penalizes mistakes and trains children to fear failure. This fear stifles creativity, innovation, and originality. Robinson argues that many education systems "educate people out of their creativity," prioritizing subjects like math and science over the arts and creating rigid hierarchies that devalue divergent thinking.

He explained:

> "We don't grow into creativity; we grow out of it. Or rather, we get educated out of it." [9]

As children progress through school, they are often taught to fear making mistakes and conform to narrow definitions of success. This stifles their innate creative potential, as they learn that creativity, imagination, and divergent thinking are less important than following rules and providing the 'right' answers.

This critique is aligned with Pablo Picasso's insight:

> All children are born artists. The problem is to remain an artist as we grow up. [9]

Children have an innate capacity for creativity, imagination, and innovation. However, as they move through traditional education systems, they are often trained to think in more linear and standardized ways, which can suppress their creative instincts. Creativity is not a luxury but a necessity for navigating the unknown.

---

9. Do Schools Kill Creativity? https://www.ted.com/talks/sir_ken_robinson_do_schools_kill_creativity?subtitle=en.

To preserve this essential skill, we must create systems and environments that celebrate exploration and originality, both in schools and in our daily lives. Whether we're parents, educators, or lifelong learners, the question we must ask is, how are we nurturing the artist, the innovator, and the risk-taker within ourselves and others?

Building Creativity: A Lifelong Journey

The beauty of creativity lies in its accessibility. It doesn't matter how old you are, where you come from, or what formal education you've received. Here are a few ways to begin:

i. Ask Questions:

Curiosity is the birthplace of creativity. Don't settle for surface-level understanding. Dig deeper into the 'why' and 'how' of the world around you. For example, think of a child staring up at the sky who asks, "Why does the sky change color?" That question could lead to becoming a scientist and discovering new phenomena.

Curiosity fuels exploration. It's what led Leonardo da Vinci to dissect human bodies in search of answers about anatomy or inspired astronomers to unravel the mysteries of the cosmos. The more questions you ask, the more connections you'll uncover, and the more opportunities you'll have to create something new.

ii. Embrace Failure:

Mistakes are not setbacks. They're stepping stones.

Thomas Edison is a perfect example. When asked about the thousands of failed attempts he made while inventing the light bulb, Edison famously said, "I have not failed. I've just found 10,000 ways that won't work." For Edison, every failed experiment wasn't a defeat but a lesson, moving him one step closer to success—his iterative process of trying, learning, and adapting ultimately brought light to the world. Imagine how different history would look if Edison had given up after his first few failures. His story teaches us that creativity isn't about instant success but rather perseverance, experimentation, and the belief that solutions exist if we're willing to seek them.

iii. Challenge Assumptions:

Creativity often begins by questioning the status quo. Ask yourself, 'What if things were done differently?' The willingness to challenge traditional thinking can unlock opportunities for innovation. Consider the Apollo 13 crisis. When an oxygen tank exploded aboard the spacecraft, engineers back on Earth were faced with the impossible challenge of bringing the astronauts home safely with limited resources. Instead of sticking to conventional solutions, they repurposed materials onboard in ways no one had ever imagined before.

This ingenious solution was only possible because the engineers dared to think differently. They questioned assumptions, worked within constraints, and turned a potential disaster into a triumph of human ingenuity.

iv. Surround Yourself with Inspiration:

Engage with diverse ideas, people, and experiences to spark new ways of thinking and learning. Creativity doesn't happen in isolation but thrives in an environment rich with diverse ideas, experiences, and people. Surround yourself with art, nature, books, or conversations that challenge your perspective and broaden your understanding.

Visit a museum and observe how artists convey stories through their brushstrokes. Take a walk through a park and observe how nature balances symmetry and chaos. Engage with people whose viewpoints differ from your own. Every new experience you encounter becomes fuel for your creative mind, sparking fresh ways of thinking and problem-solving.

v. Practice Creativity Daily:

Creativity isn't reserved for big, world-changing ideas but also for something you can practice in small, everyday ways. From journaling to brainstorming solutions for everyday problems, making creative thinking a habit.

This will train your mind to see possibilities where others see obstacles. Over time, these small acts of creative thinking build the confidence and skills needed to tackle larger challenges.

A Spark in the Darkness

Creativity is like a spark in the darkness. Though small and seemingly insignificant at first, it is powerful enough to light the way when everything else seems uncertain. Whether it's asking bold questions or challenging assumptions, every small spark of creativity builds momentum, illuminating the path forward through the unknown.

Darkness, in this context, represents the unknown. It holds challenges that overwhelm us and highlight the limitations of conventional wisdom. It's the point where rigid systems break down, where following a pre-written manual no longer suffices. In these moments, creativity shines, offering a way forward that logic alone cannot uncover. Crises are often the breeding ground for creativity. When conventional methods fail, people are forced to think differently, relying on creativity to navigate through the chaos.

During the Great Depression of the 1930s, a period marked by widespread unemployment and financial hardship, creativity brought hope and entertainment to struggling families. Charles Darrow, an unemployed salesman, created the game Monopoly to distract people from their economic woes. Darrow hand-drew the first game board on a piece of oilcloth, featuring properties named after streets in Atlantic City, New Jersey. He added play money, chance cards, and simple rules, offering players the opportunity to 'buy' and 'trade' properties, imagining a world of financial success even as they struggled to make ends meet in real life.

The game quickly gained popularity because it provided families with a fun, affordable way to pass the time and escape the weight of their financial troubles. What began as a homemade pastime soon became a cultural phenomenon. Parker Brothers eventually bought the rights to Monopoly, turning it into one of the best-selling board games of all time.

This story demonstrates how creativity and ingenuity can transform even the bleakest situations into something meaningful, positive, and enduring. Darrow's spark of creativity didn't just brighten his own life but brought light and joy to countless others, even during one of the darkest periods in modern history. This "spark in the darkness" moment demonstrates that creativity isn't just about artistic expression but is also about survival and adaptation.

The Fountain of Ideas

Creativity is like a fountain of endless, self-replenishing sources of inspiration and innovation. Unlike a finite reservoir, which diminishes with use, creativity thrives on how much you draw from it. Each idea or experience fuels the next, much like a fountain where each cascade feeds the next flow of water. This regenerative nature makes creativity one of humanity's most valuable resources, capable of solving problems, sparking innovation, and reshaping the world.

The fountain of creativity flows freely in those who allow their curiosity and imagination to expand across disciplines. Few people embody this concept better than Elon Musk, whose ideas permeate multiple industries, sparking innovation wherever they are applied.

Elon Musk's Multi-Industry Creativity

Elon Musk exemplifies the fountain of ideas. He doesn't limit his creativity to a single domain but lets it flow freely across multiple industries, challenging conventions and redefining possibilities. Some of his ingenious ventures include:

i. Tesla:

Musk reimagined the car not just as a vehicle but as an integral part of a sustainable energy ecosystem. His vision led to the popularization of electric cars, making them both practical and desirable.

ii. SpaceX:

While others saw space exploration as prohibitively expensive, Musk envisioned reusable rockets that could drastically reduce costs. SpaceX's Falcon series revolutionized the aerospace industry.

iii. Neuralink:

With Neuralink, Musk ventures into brain-machine interfaces, aiming to bridge the gap between humans and technology, address complex neurological issues, and explore the potential of human cognition.

iv. The Boring Company:

Inspired by Los Angeles' heavy traffic, Musk founded The Boring Company to develop underground tunnel systems, reimagining urban transportation.

v. OpenAI:

Musk co-founded OpenAI to explore the potential of artificial intelligence while ensuring that its development remained safe and beneficial. The organization created transformative tools, such as GPT language models, which sparked widespread interest in generative AI with the release of ChatGPT in November 2022.

What drives this endless flow of ideas? Musk's creative process is rooted in first-principles thinking, a problem-solving approach where he breaks challenges into their fundamental truths and builds solutions from the ground up. He also embraces collaboration, surrounding himself with diverse teams of experts who challenge assumptions and push boundaries.

Musk creates a fertile environment where innovation thrives by combining relentless curiosity with calculated risk-taking. But the fountain of creativity isn't exclusive to innovators like Musk. Anyone can cultivate their creative flow by feeding their curiosity, embracing experimentation, and drawing inspiration from a diverse range of sources.

Like Musk, we can all cultivate a fountain of creativity by allowing ideas from one area of our lives to inspire new possibilities in another. Creativity is not a finite resource; however, the more we utilize it, the more it grows. The key is to stay curious, take risks, and let each spark of inspiration feed the next.

Why Creativity Matters

In The Magic of Thinking Big, David J. Schwartz shares a powerful lesson inspired by Albert Einstein.

> A story is told that the great scientist Albert Einstein was once asked, How many feet are in a mile? Einstein's reply was, "I don't know. Why should I fill my brain with facts I can find in two minutes in any standard reference book?" Einstein taught us a big lesson; he thought it was more important to use your mind to think than to use it as a warehouse of facts.[10]

Einstein's point wasn't that facts don't matter; they do matter, but rather that the brain's true power lies in its ability to process, question, and create. Einstein prioritized creative problem-solving and visionary thinking over memorizing trivial details.

---

10. The Magic of Thinking Big (Audio-book) by David Schwartz, https://www.youtube.com/watch?v=-jt6v_wKK6k

"Imagination is more important than knowledge," Einstein once said. Knowledge has its limits, being confined to what is already known. Imagination, on the other hand, opens the door to infinite possibilities.

Like Einstein, we don't need to clutter our minds with easily accessible information. Instead, we should focus on freeing up mental space for big-picture thinking, asking the 'how' and 'why' instead of fixating on the 'what.'

Are you using your brain to think or to store facts?

Spark Your Creativity

Unleashing creativity starts with small, deliberate steps. This simple exercise is designed to shift your thinking and awaken your ability to see possibilities where others see limitations.

i.   Gather Five Everyday Objects:

Choose five items you interact with daily, such as:

- A spoon
- A book
- A shoelace
- A paperclip
- A water bottle

ii. Brainstorm Unconventional Uses:

For each object, think of at least three alternative ways it could be used. The goal is to push your mind beyond its usual patterns. Here are some examples:

- Spoon: A miniature garden spade, a makeshift musical instrument, or a reflector in a small solar experiment.
- Book: A doorstop, a platform to elevate a plant pot, or an emergency heat insulator in a cold room.

- Shoelace: A measuring tape, a DIY bracelet, or a way to bundle and secure items.

- Paperclip: A zipper pull, a makeshift keyring, or even a way to reset electronic devices.

- Water Bottle: A bird feeder, a weight for an improvised workout, or a funnel when cut in half.

iii. Reflect on the Process:

- Were you frustrated at first?

- Did ideas come more easily over time?

- Did you notice patterns in how you approached each object?

- What did you learn about your ability to think outside the box?

- How might this process help you tackle a challenge in your own life?

Challenging your brain to view familiar objects in unfamiliar ways helps train it to approach real-world challenges with fresh perspectives. For example, the next time you face a workplace problem, a family dispute, or a stalled project, this habit of thinking creatively can help you uncover unconventional solutions and transform obstacles into opportunities.

Think about it: Einstein's refusal to memorize trivial facts wasn't laziness; it was a deliberate choice to focus his mental energy on more profound questions and revolutionary ideas. His creativity changed the way we understand the universe, and while you don't have to revolutionize physics, you can take small steps to revolutionize the way you think.

Freddy Anzures' AHA Moment

Creativity often begins with a challenge, such as a seemingly impossible task, a system designed to trap us, or even a simple goal that demands innovation. Whether it's creating a groundbreaking phone feature or escaping an unfair situation, creativity helps us to navigate uncertainty and unlock solutions that didn't exist before.

Take the example of Freddy Anzures and Apple's iconic 'Slide to Unlock' feature. Before the iPhone's debut in 2007, phones relied heavily on physical buttons or cumbersome methods to unlock their screens. Apple aimed to create a touchscreen interface that was both secure and easy for users to interact with. Steve Jobs and his team sought a solution that would prevent accidental interactions while also feeling seamless and intuitive. It was during this time that the idea of unlocking a phone emerged in the most unusual way and at an unexpected location.

> Freddy Anzures, a user interface designer, found this idea while traveling. While in the airplane, he felt the need to relieve himself and rushed to the toilet, where he stumbled upon the mechanism to unlock the toilet washroom by sliding the knob.
>
> (Slide to Unlock)
>
> Inspired by this idea, he created a working prototype of Slide to Unlock for a touch screen. An engineer in the same team then gave this to her 3-year-old child to test it, and within seconds she successfully unlocked the phone, proving that if a 3-year-old can do it easily, this has to be 'THE SIMPLEST WAY.'[11]

"Slide to Unlock" became one of Apple's signature features and was patented as part of the iPhone's revolutionary design. Similarly, the Tale of Two Pebbles demonstrates the power of creative thinking in the face of seemingly impossible odds.

---

11. Slide to Unlock, https://www.linkedin.com/pulse/story-how-apple-got-idea-slide-unlock-parth-gohil

Tale of Two Pebbles

Once upon a time, in a small village, a farmer was in debt to a cunning and wealthy moneylender. This moneylender was not only greedy but also unscrupulous, and he had taken a liking to the farmer's beautiful daughter.

One day, the moneylender proposed a deal. "If your daughter marries me, I will forgive your debt entirely," he said.

The farmer and his daughter were horrified by the idea. Seeing their reluctance, the moneylender devised a 'fair' game to settle the matter. He proposed they meet in the village square, where he would place two pebbles, one black and one white, into a bag.

He explained, "If your daughter picks the black pebble, she will marry me, and I will forgive the debt. If she picks the white pebble, she won't have to marry me, and I'll still forgive the debt. If she refuses to pick a pebble, I'll have you thrown in jail until the debt is paid."

Though the terms seemed harsh, the farmer and his daughter agreed, feeling they had no choice. When they gathered in the square, the moneylender bent down to pick up the pebbles. The daughter, with sharp eyes, noticed that he slyly placed two black pebbles into the bag instead of one black and one white. Now she faced a seemingly impossible situation:

- If she chose a pebble, it would inevitably be black, and she would be forced to marry the moneylender.

- If she refused, her father would be jailed.

- If she exposed the cheating moneylender, he might retaliate against her family.

The daughter thought quickly. With a calm smile, she reached into the bag and pulled out a pebble. But before anyone could see what color it was, she "accidentally" dropped it onto the ground, where it became lost among the many pebbles in the square.

"Oh, how clumsy of me!" she said. "But it's easy to figure out which pebble I picked. Just look at the one still in the bag."

The moneylender, knowing he couldn't reveal that the remaining pebble was also black without exposing his deceit, had no choice but to forgive the debt and let the matter go. The farmer's daughter didn't accept the rules of the moneylender's rigged game. Instead, she reframed the situation to her advantage. By exposing his dishonesty and refusing to play by his rules, she used creativity to turn the tables. Her quick thinking teaches us several key lessons about the power of creativity:

i. Reframe the Problem:

When faced with a seemingly inescapable situation, the daughter didn't give in to despair. She looked at the problem from a new perspective, rethinking the rules of the game. Instead of choosing between two unfavorable options, she created a third path that revealed the moneylender's deceit and ensured a fair outcome.

ii. Think Beyond the Rules:

Creativity flourishes when we challenge conventional thinking. The moneylender believed he had total control because the rules were in his favor. But by 'accidentally' dropping the pebble and exposing his dishonesty, the daughter broke free from his constraints and forced him to honor the agreement.

iii. Stay Calm Under Pressure:

Even in a high-stakes situation, the daughter remained composed. Instead of panicking, she took a moment to observe, think, and act strategically. Her ability to stay calm allowed her creativity to flourish. When you are faced with challenges, take a breath, step back, and give yourself the space to think creatively.

These two stories, "Slide to Unlock" and "The Tale of Two Pebbles," show us that creativity transcends time and context. One is rooted in modern innovation, revolutionizing how we interact with technology.

The other is steeped in timeless wisdom, offering a lesson in navigating life's challenges with ingenuity. Both illustrate the universal power of creativity to solve problems, challenge systems, and create new opportunities.

Whether you're designing cutting-edge technology or navigating the complexities of daily life, creativity gives you the ability to draw your map and reshape the world around you. The one common thread between them is that neither person accepted the constraints placed before them.

Building Bridges Over Gaps

Where traditional thinking sees gaps as insurmountable obstacles, creativity envisions them as opportunities for innovation. It transforms divides into pathways, enabling the flow of ideas, collaboration, and resources. A gap is not an end but an invitation to innovate.

Picture a vast canyon separating two communities. To some, the canyon represents isolation, limitation, and impossibility. But to a creative thinker, the gap represents the difference between the current state and a future worth striving for. The bridge, whether literal or metaphorical, becomes the transformative solution that not only connects the two sides but also creates new possibilities for growth, exchange, and shared opportunity. This ability to bridge gaps is what makes creativity such a vital force in all areas of life, from education to business to personal growth. Creativity doesn't just solve problems; it creates connections that lead to progress.

Airbnb: A Bridge Between Supply and Demand

Creative thinkers have the unique ability to build bridges that link what exists today with what's possible tomorrow. One striking example of this bridge-building creativity is Airbnb. When Brian Chesky, Joe Gebbia, and Nathan Blecharczyk founded Airbnb, they saw a glaring gap in the travel and hospitality market. They noticed that travelers often struggled to find affordable, flexible accommodations, while homeowners had unused spaces.

The gap between supply (available space) and demand (travelers seeking unique lodging) was both clear and ripe for innovation. Where others might have seen this disconnect as a barrier, the Airbnb founders saw opportunity. They built a creative bridge: an online platform that connected these two groups. Through Airbnb, homeowners could rent out unused spaces, earning income in the process. Travelers, on the other hand, could find affordable, personalized, and unique lodging options.

> The story goes that Airbnb co-founders Brian Chesky, Joe Gebbia, and Nathan Blecharczyk had the idea to rent out their living room in San Francisco to conference goers who couldn't find a hotel room—and put them on an air mattress.
>
> Today, Airbnb is often used as a generic term (like how the Kleenex brand has become synonymous with tissues) for short-term rentals hosted by individuals rather than rental corporations. Far beyond the air mattresses of the early days, many Airbnbs are lavishly furnished and offer amenities that hotel rooms just can't compete with.
>
> Airbnb works by empowering anyone (well, so long as they adhere to local regulations) to rent out a room or an entire property. In the platform's early days, Airbnb hosts tended to be locals with spare rooms who wanted to make extra money on the side. Today, while many hosts are still folks with a spare room, the platform has captured the attention of real estate investors who have made Airbnbing their full-time job. [12]

This creative bridge didn't just solve a problem; it reimagined the hospitality industry and created a multi-billion-dollar market. Today, Airbnb connects millions of hosts and travelers worldwide, bridging cultural divides, building human connection, and transforming the way we think about travel.

From Spark to System

Creativity begins as a spark, a fleeting flash of inspiration that ignites when curiosity, a pressing problem, or a deep desire for change converge. This spark is the seed of possibility, but creativity's true power lies in transforming that spark into something greater: a sustainable system capable of consistently delivering value and making a lasting impact.

i.   The Spark:

Every creative journey starts with a spark. It might come as an unexpected idea during a quiet moment, a sudden realization while observing the world around you, or the convergence of unrelated thoughts that suddenly make sense together.

For example, the founders of Airbnb had a spark when they realized that travelers needed affordable accommodation and that homeowners had unused space. This simple idea carried immense potential, but like every spark, it needed nurturing and direction to thrive.

ii. The Transition:

The spark is just the beginning. To bring an idea to life, you must step into the transition phase, where deliberate effort transforms inspiration into action. Experimentation, learning, and persistence define this stage, as you refine the idea, adapt to setbacks, and shape it into a tangible form.

For instance, the founders of Airbnb didn't stop at identifying a gap in the market; they spent months refining their platform, testing their concept, and adapting to challenges.

---

12. Why Is It Called Airbnb? The Origin Story and Its Impact Today, https://www.airdna.co/blog/why-is-it-called-airbnb

They started by renting out air mattresses in their apartment to test their concept. As they refined their platform, they encountered numerous challenges, ranging from investors' doubts to logistical hurdles.

The transition is the crucible of creativity, where sparks are tested and strengthened, evolving into projects, products, or even new ways of thinking.

iii. The System:

True creativity reaches its peak when it becomes systematic. A system is more than just the outcome of a creative process; it's the foundation that ensures that creativity becomes sustainable. Systems can take many forms: a daily routine that sparks consistent innovation, a team that collaborates to execute bold ideas, or even mental habits that keep you motivated and curious.

When creativity becomes a system, it delivers consistent results aligned with your values and goals. It transforms one-time inspiration into a framework for lasting impact.

What will you do with your next moment of inspiration? Will you let it fade, or will you cultivate it into something transformative.

The master has failed more times than the beginner has even tried.

Stephen McCranie

Chapter 4

The Power of Practical Learning

Imagine a gardener tending to a vast collection of plants, each one meticulously documented in a ledger. Day after day, the gardener devotes time to memorizing the names, characteristics, and care instructions for every species. This devotion to theoretical knowledge is impressive, much like a student buried in textbooks, mastering concepts and formulas. The facts and figures are like seeds, carefully cataloged and stored in the gardener's mind, waiting for the right season to bloom.

But while the gardener is engrossed in this scholarly pursuit, the garden itself remains untended. Weeds creep through the soil, choking the growth of healthy plants. The once vibrant rows of flowers and vegetables fall into disarray, their potential wasted because the gardener has not yet put their knowledge into practice.

Knowledge, no matter how vast, is only potential energy until it is acted upon. Like seeds stored in a drawer, they need to be planted, nurtured, and given the chance to bloom. Take, for example, someone learning to drive. He might spend hours studying traffic laws and memorizing every rule. But true confidence and skill only come when he sits behind the wheel, making mistakes, stalling the engine, navigating a tricky intersection, and learning to adjust to the unpredictability of real-world conditions.

The most beautiful garden is not created by understanding plants in theory but by engaging with the soil. Feeling its texture in your hands.

Maybe a crop fails one season. Maybe pests destroy a patch of vegetables. But through these challenges, the gardener gains wisdom, becoming better equipped to succeed in the next season. What seeds have you stored in your mind, waiting to be planted? The time to tend your garden is now. Step into the soil, take action, and watch as your knowledge blooms into something extraordinary.

Experience Creates Mastery

Practical learning is the ultimate teacher. It's about getting your hands dirty and learning through action. The real world doesn't wait for you to master every concept before diving in; it demands that you jump in, make mistakes, and figure things out as you go.

Learning by doing things isn't confined to classrooms. It's out in the field, in the real world, where the best lessons are learned. Experience builds confidence, not textbooks. Imagine you want to build a fishpond. You might read about aquaculture, pH levels, and water temperatures, which is helpful theoretical knowledge. However, it's only when you start digging the pond, adjusting the water balance, observing how the fish behave, and adapting your methods based on real-world conditions that you truly begin to understand the system.

You'll make mistakes. Perhaps the water temperature is incorrect, or the pH levels disrupt the ecosystem. Each adjustment brings you closer to mastering the intricacies of your fishpond. Over time, your observations, experiments, and persistence create an ecosystem that thrives.

Just as building a fishpond requires hands-on engagement to understand its intricacies, so too does entrepreneurship. You can study business models and marketing strategies for years, but launching a business teaches you lessons that no textbook ever could. The time to act is now. Take what you know and step into the unknown. Plant something today. Build something today.

The Power of Doing

Mastery isn't born from reading books or listening to lectures. Theoretical knowledge can provide a roadmap, but it's action that takes you to the destination. It's through that navigation of the twists and turns of any creative endeavor that mastery is earned. It's not about how much you know but what you do with what you know. Start doing, start learning, and let the journey itself shape your expertise.

The Story of the Pottery Class

In a small art college, a professor teaching a pottery class decided to conduct an intriguing experiment to uncover the secrets of creativity and skill development. On the first day of the semester, he divided the students into two groups, explaining that they would be graded differently and tasked with distinct approaches to their work.

- The "Quantity" Group:

  The first group of students was informed that their grade would be determined entirely by the weight of the pots they produced. If they created 50 pounds or more of pots by the end of the semester, they would receive an A. If they made 40 pounds, they would earn a B, and so on. Essentially, their focus was to create as many pots as possible without worrying too much about perfection. The professor emphasized that their job was to experiment, get their hands dirty, and produce, produce, produce.

- The "Quality" Group:

  The second group of students was given a very different assignment. They were to create only one pot, but this pot needed to be as close to perfect as possible. Their grades would depend solely on the pot's quality, with no regard for the time or effort spent.

  These students were encouraged to plan, research, and brainstorm extensively to ensure that their single piece would meet the highest artistic standards.

At the end of the semester, the professor examined the pots from both groups. The results were surprising and even counterintuitive.

- The quantity group produced not only the most pots but also the best pots in terms of quality. Their relentless practice allowed them to learn from their mistakes, refine their techniques, and improve their craftsmanship over time. By the end of the semester, they had gained invaluable experience through hands-on action and iterative learning.
- The quality group, despite their careful planning and deliberation, produced subpar results. Their single pot lacked the refinement and polish seen in the best works from the Quantity group. This was because they spent so much time theorizing and second-guessing themselves that they didn't engage in the hands-on learning required to master their craft.

This experiment reveals a profound truth: that mastery and excellence aren't achieved through endless planning or striving for perfection. They're built through action, practice, and iteration.

Whether you're writing, painting, launching a business, or learning a new skill, the secret to progress is the same:

i. Take Action:

The more you do, the more you learn, and the closer you are to mastery.

ii. Embrace Imperfection:

Perfectionism only holds you back. Remember, every expert was once a beginner who dared to make imperfect work.

iii. Iterate to Improve:

Each attempt builds on the last. Progress is an iterative process. The first version of anything is unlikely to be perfect, but it lays the foundation for improvement.

This principle isn't confined to pottery. Some of the most successful people in history have embraced the power of doing, failing, and iterating:

- Mark Zuckerberg's Mantra:

  Zuckerberg famously said, "Move fast and break things." His approach to building Facebook emphasized speed, experimentation, and the willingness to make mistakes. By acting quickly and learning from failures, Zuckerberg's team continuously improved their platform and adapted to new challenges.

- Jeff Bezos and Experimentation:

  Jeff Bezos, founder of Amazon, once said, "If you double the number of experiments you do per year, you're going to double your inventiveness." For Bezos, success stems from taking risks, learning from failures, and iterating toward more effective solutions.

The perfect moment will never come, and no one feels entirely "ready" when they start. They start where they are, with what they have.

Confidence Through Experience

One of the most valuable byproducts of practical learning is confidence. Confidence isn't something you're born with, but it's something you build through experience. The first steps are often the hardest, filled with uncertainty, self-doubt, and the fear of failure. But with every challenge you overcome, you chip away at that fear, replacing it with confidence.

Each victory, no matter how small, builds your belief in your abilities and prepares you to tackle even bigger obstacles. Confidence isn't about knowing you'll succeed but about trusting that even if you fail, you'll learn, adapt, and try again.

Failure as a Teacher

Failure is often viewed as something to be avoided, but in reality, it's one of life's greatest teachers.

In a classroom, mistakes are often seen as final judgments, recorded in grades, and perceived as a measure of ability.

- Classroom Mindset:

  Mistakes are marked in red, and the goal is to avoid them.

- Real-World Mindset:

  Mistakes are stepping stones. Each one teaches you something new, propelling you closer to your goals.

The Feedback Loop

Practical learning operates in a feedback loop:

i.   Action Leads to Results:

   When you act, you create outcomes. Whether you succeed or fail, every result offers insight.

ii. Results Provide Feedback:

   Did your strategy work? If not, why? What could you try differently? Each result holds clues to help you refine your approach.

iii. Feedback Informs Future Action:

   Armed with what you've learned, you act. Each cycle sharpens your skills, deepens your understanding, and moves you closer to mastery.

This loop is the engine of growth.

The Builder's Toolbox

Practical learning is like gathering tools in a builder's toolbox. Each skill you acquire is another tool that empowers you to create, repair, innovate, and build the life you want. Imagine trying to build a house without a hammer or nails or wood. Would it be possible? Similarly, life's challenges often require specific skills, and without them, progress can seem out of reach. But here's the good news: tools can be acquired. Skills can be learned. And mastery can be built, piece by piece.

Take, for example, Lionel Messi, the legendary Argentine footballer and long-time icon of FC Barcelona, who exemplifies this principle. Widely regarded as one of the greatest players in football history, Messi's ability to score free kicks with precision, power, and finesse is now one of his signature skills. But this mastery didn't come naturally; it was built, piece by piece, through hard work and relentless practice.

Messi's Free-Kick Evolution

In the early stages of his career, Messi's free kick skills were relatively unremarkable. He struggled to find consistency and precision in this area. The turning point came in 2009, during a training session with the Argentina national team. Diego Maradona, a legend in his own right and the team's coach at the time, witnessed Messi taking a poorly executed free kick. Rather than criticizing him, Maradona saw potential in him. He stepped in to mentor Messi, offering personalized advice on body positioning, striking technique, and understanding the ball's movement.

At first, there were moments of frustration due to failed attempts, missteps, and inconsistency. But Messi kept practicing. Over time, his hard work paid off, and he transformed free kicks into a near-guaranteed scoring opportunity. By the early 2010s, Messi's free kick technique had become a hallmark of his game, earning him accolades and adding a new dimension to his already extraordinary skill set.

Fernando Signorini was the fitness coach for Argentina at the 2010 World Cup, and in his biography, Call to Rebellion, he sheds light on Maradona's part in Messi's development as the ultimate set-piece specialist.

'In February 2009, just a few months after Maradona took over as coach of the national team, we played a friendly against a local team in Marseille,' Signorini writes.

'We practiced the day before, and after the session, Javier Mascherano, Carlos Tevez, and Messi stayed behind for shooting practice.

Messi put the ball down and looked up at the goal slightly to his left.

When he struck the ball, it went some way over the bar to the goalkeeper's right.

He was annoyed and headed towards the dressing room, passing me as he went.

I said, "Are you going to go and shower after that rubbish? Stop getting annoyed, go and get a ball, and try again."'

Signorini says Maradona overheard the conversation, put his arm around Messi's shoulder, and embarked on a tutorial, telling Messi, 'Don't hurry the shot so much; slow your swing down, because if not, the ball does not know what you want it to do.'

Maradona demonstrated by promptly planting the ball in the top corner with Messi looking on admiringly.

Daily free-kick practice sessions after training became part of Messi's routine at Argentina and Barcelona.

'You have to practice,' Messi told Marca last year. 'It's training and habit, like any other skill.' [11]

Messi's free kick evolution is a testament to the power of adding tools to your builder's toolbox. This process of gathering tools is what transformed him into one of the most complete players in football.

---

11. How Argentina legend Diego Maradona helped crown Barcelona star Lionel Messi as the free-kick king, https://www.dailymail.co.uk/sport/football/article-6986759/How-Diego-Maradona-helped-crown-Lionel-Messi-free-kick-king.html

Building Your Skillsbox

Messi's story serves as a reminder that mastery in any field stems from identifying gaps, seeking guidance, and practicing relentlessly. Whether you're an artist refining your craft, an entrepreneur launching a new venture, or a student learning a new subject, success depends on your willingness to gather tools, adapt, and persevere. You don't need to start as an expert.

Every skill you acquire, every failure you overcome, and every lesson you absorb becomes a tool in your builder's toolbox. Ask yourself:

- What tools are you missing?

- What skills could you sharpen?

- Who could you turn to for mentorship or guidance?

Start adding to your skillsbox today, one skill at a time, and watch as your abilities grow stronger and your goals come within reach.

Cooking Without a Recipe

Practical learning is like cooking without a recipe. At first, you may not know the exact measurements or techniques, but through trial and error, you begin creating dishes that are uniquely your own. You taste, you adjust, you refine. The process isn't about following rules; it's about experimentation and innovation. Following recipes can be helpful, but they also have limits. Recipes might teach you how to replicate a dish, but they don't show you how to innovate. True mastery comes when you step beyond the instructions and trust your instincts, adapting to the ingredients you have and creating something entirely your own.

Many successful entrepreneurs and self-taught professionals embrace this philosophy. A carpenter may not have a degree but he becomes an expert through countless hours of hands-on work. A musician may never have attended a music school but has honed his craft through years of practice, jam sessions, and live performances. Cooking without a recipe reflects the messy yet rewarding journey of learning through hands-on experience.

Just as a skilled cook can create a meal from whatever ingredients he has, a self-reliant individual learns to make the best of any situation. As French culinary traditions teach: "In cooking, as in life, you are limited only by your imagination."

The Bounce of a Rubber Ball

Failure in practical learning is like dropping a rubber ball. It's not about the fall, but it's about the bounce. At first, the fall might feel like a setback, a moment of doubt or frustration. But as you rebound, you realize that every bounce makes you stronger. Each misstep teaches you how to land on your feet, turning failure into the energy that propels you forward. The world doesn't need flawless work, but it needs your work. Start building, start experimenting, start bouncing back today.

i. Act:

The sculptor doesn't start with a fully formed statue; they begin with a vision, taking hammer and chisel to the stone, chipping away until the creation emerges. Just start even small.

ii. Experience:

Embrace the challenges and mistakes. They teach you what can't be learned in theory.

iii. Reflect:

Assess what worked and what didn't. Each reflection sharpens your understanding, much like a farmer adjusting planting techniques or a chef refining their recipe.

iv. Apply:

The world rewards action, not just theory. It's through experience, through failure and success, that we become capable of creating systems that sustain us and others.

Think of your life as a canvas. Practical learning provides you with the tools and materials to create a masterpiece. Each lesson, whether it comes from a triumph or a setback, adds depth and vibrancy to your creation. The world doesn't reward untested theories or unused ideas; however, it rewards action, resilience, and the courage to learn through doing.

A Lifelong Journey

Practical learning doesn't have a finish line. As long as you're engaged with the world, there will always be new lessons to learn, new challenges to face, and new opportunities to explore. This journey of growth and discovery isn't just about what you achieve, but it's more about who you become. With every challenge you face, every skill you master, and every lesson you learn, you're not only building a life but also shaping a deeper understanding of yourself and the world around you.

Learning is like climbing a mountain range. The path is steep, sometimes grueling, and often uncertain. But with each summit you conquer, you're rewarded with a breathtaking view, one that reveals not only how far you've come but also how much further you can go. Each horizon inspires the next climb, reminding you that the journey never truly ends, and that's the beauty of it.

Ultimately, practical learning isn't just about acquiring skills or solving problems; it's about shaping your life through action, resilience, and creativity. It's about building your skillsbox, bouncing back from failure, and learning to thrive in the face of uncertainty. So, pick up your tools, roll up your sleeves, and start building. Whether it's a fishpond, a masterpiece, or an entirely new path, the world is waiting for the creations only you can bring to life.

The ladder of success is best climbed by stepping
on the rungs of opportunity.

Ayn Rand

Chapter 5

The Corporate Ladder Trap

Imagine standing at the base of a shiny, towering ladder, its rungs gleaming with the promise of success. You begin your ascent, convinced that each step upward is a move toward your dreams. At first, the climb feels exhilarating. You're rewarded for your hard work with titles, raises, and accolades.

However, as you climb higher, the rungs become wobbly under the weight of obligations, stress, relentless deadlines, and the growing pressure to conform. You start to notice invisible walls forming around you—walls crafted not from brick and mortar but from corporate policies, hierarchical structures, and unyielding expectations.

What once felt like progress now feels like a trap. The ladder you trusted to lead you to freedom and fulfillment starts to feel like a carefully constructed illusion. It might offer fleeting achievements and material comforts, but it demands something precious in return, like your time, creativity, and often, your sense of purpose. You begin to wonder if this ladder is really leading you to the life you've dreamed of, or are you merely climbing higher into a maze of stress, disillusionment, and unrelenting pressure?

The Escalator to Nowhere

The corporate ladder is often portrayed as the ultimate escalator to success, a steady, predictable pathway to stability, prestige, and financial security. From an early age, many of us are told to aspire to climb the ladder: study hard, earn a degree, secure a well-paying job, and work diligently to rise through the ranks. The narrative is straightforward: you need to climb higher, and you'll find happiness and success waiting for you at the top. But what happens when you reach the summit only to realize it's not where you want to be? What if, after all your hard work, you discover the ladder you've been climbing is leaning against the wrong wall?

Take Susan, a high-achieving marketing executive. By her mid-thirties, she had everything she thought she wanted: a corner office, a six-figure salary, and a team that admired her. From a distance, she seemed to be living her dream.

But inside, Susan felt empty. The long hours, endless meetings, and rigid expectations left her drained. Her job, which once felt like a symbol of success, had become a source of constant stress. Worse, she realized she had been chasing someone else's success, not her happiness and dreams. This isn't just Susan's story, but it's the reality for many who have sacrificed their freedom and the potential to design a life that aligns with their values and aspirations.

But what if there's another way? What if success isn't about climbing higher but about stepping off the ladder entirely? What if, instead of following a pre-designed path, you dare to create your own?

The corporate ladder, for all its promises, isn't the only option. Stepping off it can open the door to opportunities that are far more meaningful and aligned with who you are.

The Illusion of Achievement

At each rung of the ladder, we're given just enough to keep climbing in the form of a raise, a new title, or the promise of 'making it.' These milestones feel like progress, a confirmation that you're on the right path, but as you climb higher, you start to notice the costs:

i.   Freedom:

Higher positions often require more extended hours, increased stress, and reduced personal time.

ii. Creativity:

Corporate structures reward following systems, meeting KPIs, and sticking to established rules. Innovation becomes a luxury rather than a priority.

iii. Purpose:

The relentless focus on climbing the ladder can push passions and meaningful goals to the sidelines.

The ladder itself isn't inherently bad, but its design often serves the interests of the system rather than the individual. It rewards traits that keep the system running smoothly.

The desire to climb the ladder higher often turns colleagues into competitors, distorting relationships into mere transactions. Promotions become trophies rather than meaningful milestones. The higher you climb, the tighter the bonds of financial security, lifestyle dependency, and societal pressure become. This is the essence of the golden handcuffs phenomenon.

The Golden Handcuffs Phenomenon

This phenomenon occurs when your job provides so much financial stability that you become emotionally and financially dependent on it. You become trapped in a cycle where the fear of losing your income, lifestyle, and benefits overrides any desire for freedom or personal growth. Imagine wearing a pair of handcuffs crafted from pure gold.

They're beautiful, valuable, and even admired by others. But despite their allure, they're still handcuffs that are limiting your freedom, restricting your movements, and keeping you tethered to something that may no longer serve you.

Golden handcuffs don't appear overnight. They tighten gradually, often without you noticing until it feels too late to escape:

i. Rising Lifestyle Costs:

With each promotion or raise, you may upgrade your lifestyle and buy bigger houses and luxury cars and take exotic vacations. Over time, these expenses feel less like luxuries and more like necessities.

ii. Perceived Scarcity of Options:

The more specialized your role becomes, the harder it may seem to find alternative opportunities. Fear of starting over or earning less keeps you in your current position.

iii. Social Pressure:

Society often equates high-paying jobs with success. Walking away can feel like failure, even if staying means sacrificing personal happiness.

Emotional Dependency

The golden handcuffs aren't just financial; they are also emotional.

You might tell yourself, 'It's not so bad,' or 'I should be grateful for what I have.' Even as dissatisfaction grows, the idea of leaving feels like stepping into an abyss. Questions like 'What if I can't find another job?' or 'How will I support my family?' or 'What will people think?' create fear that can keep you tethered in place.

Even as dissatisfaction creeps in, the handcuffs offer a sense of comfort. They reassure you that you've built a stable life, even as they keep you from reaching for something more fulfilling.

However, while the golden handcuffs can feel inescapable, it's important to remember that they're not unbreakable.

Breaking Free from the Golden Handcuffs

Breaking free is not an abrupt leap but a deliberate process of reclaiming your freedom, step-by-step:

i. Recognize the Handcuffs:

It's easy to rationalize the trade-offs you've made for financial security, but ask yourself, 'Are you sacrificing your dreams, creativity, or well-being for a paycheck?'

ii. Redefine Security:

Proper security doesn't come from a paycheck. It comes from building systems of independence. Multiple income streams from side hustles or investments can provide the freedom you desire.

iii. Start Small:

Transitioning doesn't have to be abrupt. Begin by exploring side projects or passions while maintaining your current employment. Over time, these can evolve into sustainable systems that allow you to step away from the corporate ladder with confidence.

iv. Cultivate a Growth Mindset:

Fear of the unknown often stems from underestimating your ability to adapt. Trust in your creativity, resilience, and skills, and you will see that they're more than enough to help you succeed outside the corporate safety net.

Jeff Bezos: Building His Own Ladder

Jeff Bezos exemplifies the courage it takes to break free from the golden handcuffs. As a rising star on Wall Street, Bezos had financial security, prestige, and a promising future, but he realized that the ladder he was climbing didn't align with his potential or vision.

Early Life and Education

Jeffrey Preston Bezos, the visionary founder of Amazon, was born on January 12, 1964, in Albuquerque, New Mexico, to a teenage mother, Jacklyn Gise, and his biological father, Ted Jorgensen, who was just 19 years old at the time. When Jeff was four years old, his mother re-married Miguel Bezos, a Cuban immigrant who fled to the U.S. alone at the age of 15. Miguel adopted Jeff, and the young family moved to Houston, Texas, where Miguel worked as an engineer for Exxon. Bezos' childhood was marked by curiosity, creativity, and a knack for invention. Even as a child, he displayed an uncanny ability to think outside the box:

- He once dismantled his crib with a screwdriver to make it into a makeshift bed, a telling sign of his early problem-solving instincts.

- His parents' garage became his 'laboratory,' where he conducted science experiments, tinkered with gadgets, and let his curiosity thrive.

Academically, Bezos excelled. He graduated as valedictorian from Miami Palmetto High School, delivering a graduation speech about humanity's need to colonize space, a passion that would follow him throughout his life. He went on to attend Princeton University, where he majored in computer science and electrical engineering. Bezos graduated summa cum laude, Phi Beta Kappa, and Tau Beta Pi in 1986. His time at Princeton solidified his technical expertise, which became the foundation of his entrepreneurial ambitions.

> Valedictorian is an academic title for the highest-performing student of a graduating class of an academic institution in the United States.[12]

> Summa cum laude is an honorary title used by educational institutions to signify a degree that was earned with the highest distinction.[13]

> Phi Beta Kappa is the oldest academic honor society in the United States. It aims to promote and advocate excellence in the liberal arts and sciences and to induct outstanding students of arts and sciences at select American colleges and universities.[14]

---

12. Valedictorian, https://en.wikipedia.org/wiki/Valedictorian

13. Summa Cum Laude: Definition, Meaning, and Requirements, https://www.investopedia.com/terms/s/summa-cum-laude.asp

14. Phi Beta Kappa, https://en.wikipedia.org/wiki/Phi_Beta_Kappa

Tau Beta Pi is the oldest engineering honor society and the second oldest collegiate honor society in the United States. [15]

The Amazon Story

After graduating from Princeton, Bezos began his career in the finance sector, quickly climbing the corporate ladder. By the early 1990s, he was a vice president at D.E. Shaw & Co., a prestigious hedge fund on Wall Street. His success in the corporate world seemed assured, but Bezos began to feel restless.

In 1994, a groundbreaking statistic changed the course of his life. The internet was growing at an unprecedented rate of 2,300% per year. Bezos saw the internet not just as a tool but as a transformative platform that could revolutionize commerce. Recognizing a once-in-a-lifetime opportunity, he made the bold decision to leave his secure, high-paying job and take a calculated risk.

Bezos and his wife, MacKenzie Scott, packed their belongings into their car and drove cross-country to Seattle. During the road trip, Bezos sketched out his idea for an online bookstore, a business model that leveraged the internet's scale and reach. Books, he realized, were the perfect product for e-commerce due to their universal appeal and vast inventory.

Amazon.com launched in 1995 from Bezos' garage, named after the world's largest river to reflect his ambition for growth and dominance.

The site's tagline, Earth's Biggest Bookstore, hinted at Bezos' grand vision: a company that would eventually become a marketplace for virtually everything.

---

15. Tau Beta Pi, https://en.wikipedia.org/wiki/Tau_Beta_Pi

Early Challenges

Bezos faced significant skepticism in Amazon's early days.

- Investors doubted the viability of an online bookstore, with many questioning whether customers would be willing to buy books or anything else over the internet.

- The business initially operated on razor-thin margins, reinvesting most of its profits into growth and innovation, a strategy that drew criticism from Wall Street analysts who were focused on short-term profitability.

Despite these challenges, Bezos remained committed to his long-term vision of making Amazon "Earth's most customer-centric company." His strategy centered on reinvention and an obsessive focus on customer experience, which eventually became the bedrock of Amazon's success.

Innovation and Growth

Over time, Bezos proved his critics wrong. Amazon evolved far beyond its origins as an online bookstore, becoming one of the most innovative and dominant companies in the world. Bezos pioneered numerous innovations that reshaped entire industries:

i. 1-Click Shopping:

    Streamlining the online shopping process and making it faster and more user-friendly.

ii. Amazon Prime:

    A subscription service that redefined customer loyalty by offering fast delivery, streaming, and other benefits.

iii. Kindle:

    Revolutionizing how people read by making eBooks accessible and convenient.

iv. Amazon Web Services (AWS):

Turning cloud computing into a multibillion-dollar business, providing the backbone for countless websites and applications.

Amazon's strategy of reinvesting profits into innovation, technology, and infrastructure allowed it to expand into diverse sectors, including electronics, clothing, groceries, and even artificial intelligence.

Today, at the time of writing, Amazon dominates e-commerce, cloud computing, logistics, and more, with a valuation exceeding $1 trillion.

Beyond Amazon

Jeff Bezos' ambitions didn't stop with Amazon. In 2000, he founded Blue Origin, a private aerospace company dedicated to making space travel accessible and sustainable. This endeavor was inspired by the same passion for space that drove his high school graduation speech decades earlier.

Bezos' vision for Blue Origin is to create a future where millions of people live and work in space, preserving Earth's resources while expanding humanity's horizons.

The company's reusable rocket, New Shepard, is a key milestone toward making space tourism a reality, while long-term plans include building human habitats in space.

Jeff Bezos epitomizes the idea of breaking free from the golden handcuffs. He could have stayed in his lucrative Wall Street career, climbing someone else's ladder. Instead, he chose to build his own, one that didn't just lead upward but outward.

From tinkering with science experiments in his parents' garage to revolutionizing global commerce and exploring space, Bezos embodies the power of boldness, vision, and action. His story serves as a reminder that success can be found by having the courage to step into the unknown and create something entirely new.

Borrowing Someone Else's Ladder

Climbing a corporate ladder is like borrowing someone else's tool. It might help you move upward, but you're not in control of where it leads. Here's another story: Mike was a marketing manager who worked tirelessly to advance in his company. He achieved the title of director, but as the demands of his role grew, he realized he was building a vision that wasn't his own. His passion for writing, something he had once cherished, faded into the background. Deadlines, the balanced scorecard, and endless meetings had replaced creativity and passion.

Then, one day, the ladder crumbled. A sudden company restructuring left Mike without a job. It was only then, as he stood at the bottom looking up, that he realized that the ladder he had climbed wasn't his own. He had spent years building someone else's vision and ignoring his own.

Mike was just another part of a vast assembly line, where each worker contributed to building a product that might never reflect their artistry.

Climbing Toward Someone Else's Vision

Corporate systems are designed to reward you for advancing their vision, not yours. Promotions, raises, and titles are incentives that motivate you to move forward.

Let me remind you about the classic 'carrot and stick' metaphor. Think of a cart driver who is attempting to drive a reluctant horse. The driver dangles a carrot in front of the horse to entice it forward while holding a stick to enforce compliance. The carrot represents the promise of rewards, such as raises, bonuses, and titles. At the same time, the stick symbolizes the consequences of failing to meet expectations, including performance reviews, job insecurity, or missed opportunities.

In this system, the carrot may seem appealing at first, but its purpose isn't to satisfy the horse; it's to keep it moving toward the driver's destination. Similarly, in a corporate structure, the rewards you chase often align with the organization's goals, not your own. The stick, whether it's the threat of being overlooked for promotions or the fear of job instability, ensures compliance and keeps you tethered to their vision.

Here's what happens when you rely on a borrowed ladder:

i.   Lack of Ownership:

Decisions about your role and future are often made by those who own the system, leaving you only one option: to obey.

ii. Misaligned Goals:

Instead of working toward your passions, you're focused on achieving goals set by the organization, which may not align with what you truly value.

iii. Dependency on the System:

Your income, growth, and professional identity are tied to the organization's success. A single decision from higher up, like a layoff, restructuring, or a policy change, can derail years of progress.

iv. Creativity Suppression:

Conformity and predictability are often valued over innovation, leaving little room for self-expression or new ideas.

v.   Loss of Passion:

Pursuing promotions and accolades often overshadows personal fulfillment, leaving you disconnected from your true interests and aspirations.

Building Your Own Ladder

We all have the power to reclaim our journeys. Instead of climbing someone else's ladder, you can craft your own, a ladder built from the materials of your personal experiences, unique talents, and heartfelt aspirations. Every rung can reflect the vibrant colors of your dreams rather than the muted tones of corporate expectations.

Building your ladder is like designing your fishpond. You become the builder and caretaker of a thriving ecosystem, nurturing different dreams and ventures. Each fish represents a passion project or income stream—a small side hustle that could blossom into something more meaningful, or a creative endeavor that reignites your imagination. This process is not just about financial independence but about creating a life that feels authentic to you.

Let Go of Fear and Embrace the Waves

Stepping off the corporate ladder can feel intimidating. The ladder, although confined, offers a sense of stability, but stability isn't the same as freedom. Let go of the fear that leaving its comfort will lead to chaos. Instead, think of life as a surfer riding the waves. The ups and downs may seem unpredictable, but they are also exhilarating. Each rise and fall becomes an opportunity to learn, adapt, and evolve. Surges in income and success may ebb and flow, but this rhythm is a part of building something meaningful, an experience that enriches your story and connects you to your passions. The beauty of owning your ladder lies in the freedom to choose your direction and the courage to embrace the uncertainty that fuels growth.

The Freedom of Owning Your Ladder

I will introduce the metaphor of a bird in a gilded cage in the next chapter. Its colorful plumage symbolizes its potential, but its wings are confined, unable to explore the vast sky beyond. The corporate ladder often feels like this cage—safe, predictable, and adorned with corporate perks and titles. But the price of safety is the loss of freedom. The bird is fed with breadcrumbs of recognition, its songs muted by the hum of office politics.

When you design your ladder, you break free from the constraints of someone else's vision and reclaim agency over your life. What owning your ladder gives you:

i. Where It Leads:

You define the destination, aligning your goals with your passions and values, and not someone else's corporate agenda.

ii. How You Climb:

You set the pace and direction of your growth, adjusting as your priorities evolve. Whether you build slowly or take bold leaps, the choice is yours.

iii. What You Gain:

The rewards, whether financial, creative, or otherwise, are yours to keep, invest, and share on your terms.

When you build your ladder, you sculpt your own identity. Like a skilled craftsman, each rung you add is a testament to your imagination.

Allow your passions to guide you. When you embrace the joy of autonomy and the thrill of unpredictability, you'll find that the most significant rewards often lie not in the ascent but in the freedom to chart your course.

The world is full of ladders, but only the one you build can take you where you truly want to go. Start today. Lay the foundation, craft the rungs, and embrace the journey of becoming the architect of your destiny.

Universities are like fishing schools, churning out skilled anglers each year but without ponds to fish in.

Chapter 6

The System of Independence

The Leap into Independence

Picture a bird perched on the edge of its nest, its wings outstretched, gazing out at the expanse of sky before it. The nest, once a sanctuary that sheltered it from storms and predators, has now become a constraint. To truly live, the bird must leap into the unknown, spread its wings, and embrace the freedom of the skies.

Independence is the moment when the bird takes that leap, not with certainty, but with courage. It's the point where reliance on the safety of the nest gives way to self-reliance. Like that bird, we all face moments when comfort becomes a form of confinement.

The "nest" may be a secure but unfulfilling job, a system that dictates your limits, or a predictable routine that no longer allows you to grow. Though comfort zones provide safety, they come with hidden baggage:

i.   They limit growth:

Keeping you small and dependent.

ii. They suppress creativity:

They stifle your ambition and the exploration of your potential.

iii. They deny freedom:

They prevent you from experiencing the freedom and fulfillment that come from autonomy.

The leap into independence is a bold decision to build your system of security and opportunity, rather than waiting for others to provide it for you. You create a framework where your efforts, decisions, and creativity drive your stability and growth.

This framework is your fishpond, a system that sustains you, provides value, and gives you control over your life. Building your fishpond is a declaration of that freedom. It is the act of stepping away from any dependency, whether on an employer, a system, or societal expectations, and creating something that allows you to thrive indefinitely.

Like the bird, you were never meant to stay in the nest forever. You were meant to fly. The bird that leaps discovers that the sky is not to be feared, but it is where it was always meant to be. Likewise, when you take the leap into independence and begin owning your fishpond, you realize the nest was just a stepping stone to something far greater.

The Fishpond: A Blueprint for Independence

A fishpond is more than just a metaphor; it's a framework for self-reliance and sustainability, a system of independence and sustainable value. Unlike the borrowed ladders and external systems that limit your potential, a fishpond is yours to create, maintain, grow, and enjoy the benefits. In this system:

- The fish represent income streams, creative projects, or the opportunities you generate.
- The maintenance reflects the effort, skills, and ingenuity required to keep the pond thriving.
- The pond itself symbolizes your ecosystem, a self-sustaining structure where you control every aspect of your success.

Owning a fishpond means embracing responsibility, but it also means claiming the freedom to decide how to live and work. It's the antithesis of dependence on someone else's system, where your growth is constrained by rules you didn't create. When you own a fishpond, you take control of your destiny. You decide:

i. The Rules:

You set all the terms, including how you operate, what you charge, and how you allocate your resources. You're no longer bound by someone else's schedule, policies, or limitations.

ii. The Growth:

You control the size and scale of your pond. Do you want to expand it into a vast, thriving ecosystem with multiple income streams and ventures? Or do you prefer a smaller, more manageable pond that offers balance and flexibility? The choice is yours.

iii. The Rewards:

You reap the benefits of your effort, rather than receiving benefits handed out by others who 'own' the system.

This is the antithesis of dependence on traditional systems, where others dictate your opportunities:

i. Restricted Access:

You can only fish during designated hours (your work schedule).

ii. Limited Rewards:

No matter how hard you work, your 'catch' is often capped by predetermined rules like your salary, bonuses, or position. The system ensures that the bulk of the value you create benefits the owners, not you.

iii. Bounded Growth:

Even with hard work, your advancement depends on others' decisions or office politics, company priorities, or structural hierarchies.

The choice is simple:

- Will you continue fishing in ponds owned by others, subject to their rules and limitations?
- Or will you build your fishpond, where you create the rules, decide the growth, and reap the rewards?

Schools of Fishing

Universities and traditional education systems can be likened to fishing schools. Here, students learn the theories, techniques, and strategies of fishing. They master the mechanics, such as choosing the right rods, bait, and casting techniques to catch the largest fish. These lessons are valuable, providing foundational knowledge and discipline, much like a well-crafted fishing manual. However, there's a glaring oversight: most fishing schools stop at teaching. They rarely equip students with access to the fishponds, the opportunities, the systems, and the practical environments where their skills can be applied to create value and sustain themselves. No thriving waters are waiting for students to cast their lines, nor are there guarantees of fish-filled ponds or opportunities.

Each year, thousands of newly minted "trained fishers," graduates armed with shiny, beautifully crafted fishing hooks in the form of academic qualifications like certificates, diplomas, degrees, and master's degrees. These hooks symbolize their hard-earned knowledge. However, instead of being directed to thriving, bountiful waters, graduates are released into vast, barren deserts. The job market is oversaturated and highly competitive, with scarce opportunities that quickly run dry.

The Knowledge-Opportunity Gap

Picture this: a group of graduates standing on the edge of a vast desert. Each holds a beautifully polished hook, confident in the skills they've acquired. But when they cast their lines, the hooks land in the sand. There are no fish, no ponds, and no system to connect their expertise to real-world opportunities. This is the stark reality for many:

- Underemployment:

    A software engineering graduate is working as a data entry clerk because relevant jobs are scarce.

- Mismatched Roles:

   A finance major managing a retail store because their chosen field is oversaturated with similar degrees.

The issue isn't with the hooks (their qualifications) or even the lessons taught in fishing schools (the theories and techniques). The problem lies in the knowledge-opportunity gap, a disconnect between the education system and the real-world environments where this knowledge can create value.

Imagine a fisherman who has mastered every casting technique, understands every nuance of bait selection, and has studied the migration patterns of fish for years. On paper, they are the epitome of expertise. But take away the lakes and ponds where they can apply this knowledge, and their expertise becomes little more than abstract theory. The potential is there, but it remains unrealized.

Education succeeds when students can sustain themselves in practice, not just in theory. The actual test lies not in how well someone can 'cast a line in theory' but in their ability to build systems of value in the real world.

The Illusion of Bigger Nets

Faced with this disconnect, many graduates respond by acquiring more qualifications, each more prestigious and specialized than the last. They believe that building the most extensive and intricate fishing net, or obtaining the shiniest fishing rod, will guarantee them success. The shiny rod or the expansive net becomes a symbol of their aspirations, a culmination of their hard work, and their trust in the promise of traditional education that the more you learn, the more valuable you become.

A larger or more intricate net may look impressive, but its effectiveness depends on where and how it's cast.

- A graduate with three master's degrees in unrelated fields might have a vast net but lack focus, making it difficult to position themselves as an expert in any domain.
- A graduate with a single degree and hands-on experience might have a smaller net but can cast it strategically, targeting specific opportunities.

In today's job market, the oversaturation of degrees and certifications has diminished their once-perceived value. This overcrowding shifts the focus from what you know to what you can do with what you know. It's no longer about the size of the net but how well you've prepared yourself to find and create opportunities.

Shiny Rods and Expansive Nets

In fishing schools, students are taught to value the size and quality of their tools, the rods, nets, and hooks they use. The more polished and prestigious your "fishing gear," the more capable you're perceived to be. But the truth is, a shiny fishing rod is useless if the pond is barren.

Look it this way:

- A fisherman with the latest, most advanced rod will still fail to catch anything if the waters they fish in are shallow or overcrowded.
- Conversely, a fisherman with a basic rod and a creative mindset can succeed by finding new fishing spots, building their ponds, or learning to fish in overlooked waters.

In today's world, it's not the size of the net or the shine of the rod that determines success, but it's the ability to think differently, adapt to changing conditions, and create opportunities where none exist.

The Desert as the Job Market

The desert, with its endless stretches of barren land, symbolizes the stark realities of today's job market. It's an unforgiving landscape shaped by scarcity, fierce competition, endless wandering, and systemic barriers.

- Sparse Opportunities:

  Like oases scattered across miles of barren sand, meaningful and well-paying jobs are few and far between. Many industries have limited entry points, leaving graduates searching tirelessly for roles that align with their skills and aspirations.

- Harsh Conditions:

  Economic instability, automation, and systemic inequalities make the job market even more challenging. Many employers demand prior experience, creating a frustrating cycle where fresh graduates face rejection because they lack the one thing they haven't yet had the chance to gain: hands-on experience.

- Endless Wandering:

  Many graduates transition from one temporary job to another, seeking a more stable and fulfilling role. They become trapped in a state of survival, working at jobs that do not align with their skills or passions.

From Credentials to Creativity

The job market may be a desert, but it doesn't have to be a dead end. Those who dare to think beyond the overcrowded ponds and are willing to adapt can discover hidden opportunities and create their fishponds.

Shift your perspective. Instead of focusing solely on collecting bigger and better nets, ask yourself:

i.   How can I use what I already have to explore uncharted waters?

ii. What gaps exist in the market that I can fill with my unique skills?

iii. How can I pivot to create opportunities, even in barren conditions?

The desert may seem barren, but for those who dare to explore, it holds hidden opportunities. Will you wander aimlessly, hoping for an oasis, or will you start building your fishpond? The choice is yours.

Fishing Hooks Without Ponds

The other fundamental problem is that fishing schools rarely teach students how to create opportunities for themselves. For instance, engineering graduates may leave university with an impressive understanding of fluid dynamics or circuit design. But if no company hires them, they may find themselves stuck, unsure how to translate their skills into meaningful opportunities.

Without entrepreneurial tools, a creative mindset, or the ability to identify and fill market gaps, these graduates are like expert fishermen stranded in a desert with beautifully crafted fishing hooks but no fishponds to catch fish.

Fishing schools often condition individuals to seek opportunities rather than create them. The job market becomes the sole focus of their ambitions. Yet, when jobs are unavailable due to economic downturns, automation, or oversaturation in specific fields, graduates feel stranded.

Their potential, like unused hooks, remains unrealized. This systemic issue highlights the importance of independence and creativity. It's not enough to rely on someone else's fishpond. To thrive, you must build your own. Few stories illustrate this principle better than Jack Ma's journey.

The Story of Jack Ma and Alibaba's Global Success

Jack Ma is a global icon of entrepreneurship, leadership, and innovation. As the founder of Alibaba Group, one of the world's largest e-commerce companies, Jack Ma's extraordinary journey from a modest background to becoming one of the wealthiest and most influential individuals is truly inspirational.

Humble Beginnings

Born in Hangzhou, China, in 1964, Jack Ma grew up in poverty. His childhood was shaped by scarcity but also by an insatiable curiosity and a passion for learning.

i. A Passion for Learning:

    From a young age, Jack displayed an insatiable curiosity and a strong desire to learn, despite academics not being his strong suit. He was drawn to languages and communication, a trait that would later define his leadership style.

ii. Learning English on His Own:

    Jack Ma took an unconventional approach to learning English. Every morning for eight years, he would ride his bicycle to a hotel in Hangzhou to offer free tours to foreign tourists in exchange for practicing English. He built relationships with people from around the world and even acquired the name 'Jack' from a tourist who found his real name hard to pronounce.

iii. Repeated Failures in Education:

    Jack Ma faced many academic struggles, failing his middle school and college entrance exams multiple times. Despite his persistence, he was rejected from universities twice before finally gaining acceptance to Hangzhou Teachers' Institute, a small local college.

    Jack's academic challenges didn't deter him. Instead, they instilled in him a relentless determination to keep trying, an attitude that would become his guiding principle throughout his career.

Facing Rejection in His Early Career

After graduating, Jack Ma encountered significant rejection in the job market, which could have easily broken his spirit.

i. 30 Job Rejections:

    Jack applied for 30 different jobs and was rejected by all of them. Even when KFC came to Hangzhou to hire, 24 out of 25 candidates were accepted, but Jack was the only one rejected.

ii. No Technical or Business Background:

Jack Ma had no expertise in technology or computers, which would later make his foray into tech entrepreneurship even more surprising.

The Internet Sparks a Vision

In 1995, Jack Ma visited the United States and encountered the internet for the first time.

This experience changed his life:

- Jack Ma searched the word "beer" and found pages from all over the world except China.
- Realizing China's absence on the internet, he recognized an opportunity to bring his country into the digital age.

Ma began building websites for Chinese companies with the help of friends in the United States. He said that "the day we got connected to the Web, I invited friends and TV people over to my house," and on a very slow dial-up connection, "we waited three and a half hours and got half a page," he recalled. "We drank, watched TV, and played cards, waiting. But I was so proud. I proved the Internet existed."[16]

Despite lacking technical skills or computer knowledge, Jack Ma was captivated by the internet's potential. It sparked his entrepreneurial vision to create a digital platform that could connect Chinese businesses with the world.

The Birth of Alibaba

In 1999, Jack Ma gathered 17 friends in his small apartment and pitched his vision for an online platform that would help small businesses in China access global markets.

---

16. Jack Ma, https://en.wikipedia.org/wiki/Jack_Ma

That meeting marked the beginning of Alibaba.com.

- The Early Struggles:

  Alibaba faced skepticism from investors, who doubted the feasibility of e-commerce in China's underdeveloped internet infrastructure.

- Customer-Centric Innovation:

  Jack Ma's vision was rooted in helping small businesses thrive. While competitors focused on profits, Alibaba prioritized its users, creating solutions that addressed their pain points.

- Beating Global Competitors:

  When eBay entered China, many believed Alibaba wouldn't stand a chance. However, Ma saw the power of local adaptation. He focused on understanding Chinese consumers and their needs, ultimately driving eBay out of the Chinese market.

- Financial Uncertainty:

  In Alibaba's early days, the company faced funding issues.

- Building Trust with AliPay:

  In the early 2000s, Chinese consumers were skeptical of online payments. To address this issue, Alibaba introduced Alipay, an escrow service that ensures secure transactions. Despite criticism, Alipay became a massive success, transforming digital payments in China.

The Global Impact of Alibaba

Under Jack Ma's leadership, Alibaba became a tech giant, transforming e-commerce, logistics, cloud computing, and finance. Its global platforms, such as AliExpress, Taobao, and Tmall, serve millions of users worldwide, empowering both businesses and consumers. Alibaba's success also inspired a new generation of entrepreneurs in China and beyond.

Own Thy Fishpond

Are you waiting for someone to lead you to a pond, only to find it shallow, overcrowded, or empty? Or will you take the initiative to explore new lands and create your fishpond, one that sustains you, reflects your unique vision, and puts you in control of your future?

You don't have to keep casting your line into barren sands or rely on someone else's system for success. The power to create your thriving ecosystem of value is entirely within your reach.

How do you begin building your fishpond?

i. Identify Your Resources:

The foundation of any thriving fishpond begins with recognizing and appreciating the resources you already possess. While these resources might not always seem obvious at first glance, they will form the bedrock of your potential ecosystem. These assets include your skills, hobbies, networks, time, and even your unique life experiences, all of which can be leveraged to create value.

Start by conducting a self-assessment, asking yourself:

- What am I naturally good at?
- What do I enjoy doing in my free time?
- What problems do people often ask me to solve?
- What skills or knowledge have I gained through my life experiences or work?

Take a moment to list, say, four skills, hobbies, or areas of expertise where you feel confident or passionate. The key is to align your natural abilities with opportunities to create value.

Examples of Identifying and Monetizing Resources:

a. Writing:

o Offer freelance writing services.

o Start a niche blog or publish a newsletter.

- o Provide ghostwriting services for authors, entrepreneurs, or professionals.

b. Cooking:

- o Start a catering service for busy professionals.
- o Launch a YouTube channel with easy-to-follow cooking tutorials.
- o Write and sell recipe eBooks or meal prep guides.

c. Design:

- o Offer graphic design services for logos, branding, or social media content.
- o Sell customizable design templates (e.g., Canva templates, website themes, or digital invitations).
- o Create design courses on platforms like Udemy or Skillshare.

d. Speaking:

- o Host a podcast on a niche topic or area of expertise.
- o Offer motivational speaking services for events, schools, or businesses.
- o Run workshops on communication, leadership, or public speaking skills.

ii. Choose Your Fish:

The "fish" in your fishpond represent the income streams or value-driven outputs that sustain your system. These income streams should align with your resources, passions, and skills while offering value to others. Start small, test your ideas, and gradually expand your efforts. Examples of Fish (Income Streams):

a. Freelance Work:

- o Use platforms like Upwork, Fiverr, or LinkedIn to offer your skills in writing, consulting, design, photography, or tutoring.

b. Online Courses or Workshops:

- o Share your expertise by creating digital courses on platforms like Udemy, Coursera, or Skillshare.

- o Host in-person or virtual workshops for specific audiences, such as entrepreneurs, students, or creatives.

c. Selling Physical or Digital Products:

- o Sell handmade crafts, art, or merchandise through platforms like Etsy or Shopify.

- o Develop and sell digital products such as eBooks, stock photos, templates, or software tools.

d. Content Creation:

- o Start a blog, podcast, or YouTube channel centered on your niche and monetize through ads, sponsorships, or premium content subscriptions.

- o Leverage platforms like Patreon to offer exclusive content to paying members.

Choose "fish" that are not only profitable but also sustainable and enjoyable. The more aligned they are with your skills and passions, the easier it will be to maintain them in the long term.

iii. Build and Maintain the Ecosystem:

A fishpond isn't built overnight. Like any thriving ecosystem, it requires consistent care, adaptability, and growth. The key to long-term success lies in striking a balance between effort and sustainability while remaining adaptable to both challenges and opportunities.

Tips to Build and Maintain Your Fishpond:

a. Stay Relevant:

Keep up with trends and market demands in your field.

- o Example: A freelance graphic designer might learn new tools like AI design software to stay competitive.

- o Action: Follow industry news, take online courses, or join professional forums.

b. Refine Your Skills:

Treat your skills like assets that grow in value with continuous improvement. Invest in continuous self-improvement through learning and practice.

- o Example: A blogger could learn search engine optimization (SEO) to attract higher-paying clients looking for content that ranks on Google.

- o Action: Attend webinars, take courses, or read books to master the latest trends and tools related to your field.

c. Consistency is Key:

Treat your fishpond like a garden that requires regular watering, pruning, and care. Consistency builds trust, attracts opportunities, and ensures steady growth.

- o Example: A content creator who posts videos every Monday can build an audience that looks forward to their work, increasing loyalty and engagement.

- o Action: Set schedules, create routines, and stick to them even when growth feels slow.

d. Adapt to Challenges:

Challenges are inevitable, but they are also opportunities to pivot and innovate.

- o Example: If one of your income streams (e.g., freelance work) slows down, shift focus to expanding another, like digital product sales or consulting.

- o Action: Regularly assess what's working and what isn't. Be open to exploring new ideas and be willing to pivot when necessary.

e. Measure Progress:

Track your growth, set goals, and celebrate milestones. Routinely evaluate what's working and what isn't.

- o Example: If your blog attracts 500 monthly visitors, set a goal to increase traffic by 20% through SEO and social media sharing.

- o Action: Use tools like Google Analytics, income trackers, or project planners to evaluate your performance.

Fishpond Harvest

Owning a fishpond represents more than just personal success but a thriving ecosystem that offers endless opportunities to create value for yourself and your community. Each harvest extends beyond sustenance, symbolizing the abundance and flexibility that comes with ownership and innovation. You can leverage your system's potential to support, empower, and collaborate with others while unlocking its full versatility.

Harvesting the full potential of your fishpond:

i. Food for You and Your Family:

At its most basic level, your fishpond provides nourishment and security for you and your loved ones. It provides a dependable supply of essentials, whether that's financial stability, emotional fulfillment, or creative freedom.

For example, a small-scale organic farmer grows vegetables for his family but also involves his children in learning sustainable farming practices, passing on knowledge and instilling a sense of independence. This ensures nourishment for today and independence for tomorrow.

ii.   Sell Surplus:

When your fishpond begins to thrive, it often produces more than you need. This surplus becomes an opportunity to generate additional income or value by sharing your abundance with others.

- A woodworking hobbyist who enjoys crafting tables, chairs, and decorative items. Once they've filled his home, he starts selling these pieces online through platforms like Etsy or at craft fairs.

- A home cook who experiments with recipes turns her surplus meals into a profitable side hustle by offering meal delivery services using platforms like Uber Eats or Mr. D.

iii. Charge People to Fish:

When you own a fishpond, you can create systems that benefit others while compensating you for access. Charging others to fish becomes a way to monetize the resources you've cultivated.

- Passionate photographers can rent out studios to other photographers and creators, monetizing downtime and by so doing, creating an additional income stream.
- A programmer who builds useful APIs or tools can charge developers for usage access, generating recurring revenue.

Charging people to fish allows you to maximize the value of your fishpond. The pond becomes a shared space where you set the terms for access, ensuring mutual benefit without losing ownership.

iv.   Train People to Fish:

Teaching others how to fish transforms your knowledge into a valuable resource. When you mentor, coach, or train others, you not only create income opportunities but also empower people to build their systems.

- Coaching and Consulting: Offer personalized advice to individuals looking to build their fishponds.

- Online Courses: Package your techniques into structured learning modules for platforms like Udemy or Skillshare.

- Workshops and Seminars: Host virtual or in-person events to teach specialized skills or share valuable knowledge.

v. Train People How to Create Fishponds:

Once you've mastered your system, others will naturally look to you for guidance. Beyond teaching people how to fish, you can empower them to build their self-sustaining systems.

Your pond becomes a source of inspiration and expansion, catalyzing a network of ponds that enriches the entire ecosystem.

- A successful entrepreneur can launch an incubator program to mentor aspiring business owners, providing them with the tools and resources to succeed.

- A property owner can help others to create their rental income streams by teaching real estate investment strategies.

vi. You Determine Your Net Worth:

Owning a fishpond puts you in control of your value. A paycheck or employer no longer dictates your worth. Instead, it reflects the systems you've built, the value you've created, and the effort you've invested.

- A freelance writer negotiates rates and picks clients, escaping the limits of corporate pay scales.

vii. Collaborate and Expand:

Beyond ownership, your fishpond becomes a platform for collaboration. Partnering with others can expand your ecosystem, creating opportunities for shared value and collective growth. It becomes a hub for creative alliances and strategic partnerships that expand its potential for success.

- A musician can collaborate with other artists, pooling talent to create a joint album, thereby growing both their audiences.

- A tech developer can partner with a designer to create a visually stunning app, combining their joint expertise for greater success.

viii. You Can Fish Anytime; Even Naked in the Middle of the Night:

The ultimate benefit of owning a fishpond is the freedom and autonomy it provides. No rules or external limitations are dictating when, where, or how you access your resources. You own your time, your opportunities, and your creative process.

- A digital nomad running an online business works from anywhere in the world at any hour.

- Writers can spend quiet, late nights working on a passion project, knowing that they control their timeline and creative direction.

The choice is clear: compete for fish in overcrowded ponds or build your own. By owning your fishpond, you control your resources, create opportunities, and design a system that is uniquely yours that will then sustain you and others.

Obstacles are like missing pieces of a puzzle; finding and fitting them completes the picture of your success.

Chapter 7

Facing the Storms

The Storm: A Catalyst for Growth

Every journey to success will encounter its fair share of storms. These storms can feel overwhelming, threatening to uproot everything you've built, but just as a sailor learns to navigate turbulent seas, your ability to face and weather challenges defines the strength of your foundation.

Imagine standing by your fishpond as dark clouds gather overhead. The winds howl, and the rain pelts the surface of the water, disturbing its calm. At first, the storm feels destructive, a force working against you. But as the rain subsides, you notice how it replenishes the pond, washing away debris and nourishing the soil. Storms aren't the end of the journey but are essential to it. They push you to adapt, innovate, and grow in ways calm waters never could.

These storms take many forms, including financial difficulties, personal struggles, the doubts of others, or unexpected life events. Success isn't about avoiding these storms. It's about embracing them as necessary catalysts for transformation. Every drop of rain, every gust of wind, contributes to the strength of your fishpond, preparing you for even greater opportunities ahead.

Seeing Opportunity in the Storm

Storms are not just tests of endurance but are also opportunities in disguise. They shake up routines, disrupt comfort zones, and force you to reassess, adapt, and innovate. While calm waters may lull you into complacency, storms demand action. They expose vulnerabilities, create urgency, and push you to think differently. Without turbulence, the opportunity for growth might go unnoticed.

Look at this:

- A financial crisis might force you to reevaluate your spending, explore new income streams, or even discover a more sustainable way to live.

- A failed business idea might uncover gaps in your strategy or inspire a fresh, innovative approach that you hadn't considered.

- A personal setback, whether it's a relationship ending, a career detour, or a health challenge, can teach you resilience and remind you of what truly matters in life.

Storms push you to break old patterns and explore new ways of thinking. What feels like destruction is often the necessary clearing of space for new growth to emerge. Whenever you encounter a storm, ask yourself:

- What can this storm teach me?

- What weaknesses is it exposing, and how can I address them?

- What opportunities might it bring that I hadn't considered before?

The Rainbow After the Storm

Rain is often seen as an inconvenience. It darkens skies, disrupts plans, and leaves the ground muddy. But rain is also life-giving. Without it, rivers would dry up, crops would wither, and ecosystems would collapse. In much the same way, challenges might be inconvenient, but they nourish your potential. They force you to rise to the occasion, building strength and clarity for the road ahead. Think of the promise that follows every storm.

The rainbow arching across the sky and the vibrant, greener world left behind. The storm's chaos clears away stagnation, and the rain revitalizes the soil, laying the foundation for new growth. Similarly, every challenge you face carries a hidden reward.

Resilience in the Face of Adversity

Those who succeed are not the ones who avoid hardship but those who face it head-on, using each setback as a stepping stone toward their goals. They know that a challenge is often what separates those who succeed from those who give up. When setbacks occur, your perspective determines the outcome.

If you view failure as a dead end, it can paralyze you. But when you see it as a detour, a chance to learn and improve, you can transform a challenge into an opportunity for growth. Each challenge becomes a weight in the gym of life. The more you lift, the stronger you become. Consider an entrepreneur who faces rejection time and again when pitching his idea. Each 'no' sharpens his pitch, refines his strategy, and strengthens his resolve.

By the time he succeeds, he will have transformed into a seasoned professional. So, the next time the winds howl and the rain falls, don't fear the storm. Embrace it. Remember, after all, every storm carries the promise of a rainbow.

Challenges and Solutions in Building Your Systems

Building your fishpond is a challenging and rewarding journey. Obstacles, though daunting, aren't meant to stop you. Like a seedling growing into a sturdy tree, you'll face winds, pests, and droughts, but these trials are what strengthen your roots and help you thrive.

i. Problem:
Initial Lack of Resources or Clarity:

Before your fishpond is built, the process of identifying and utilizing your resources can feel overwhelming. Many people face the challenge of not recognizing the value in what they already possess, like their skills, time, networks, or life experiences.

At the heart of this challenge lies self-doubt. The quiet but persistent voice that whispers, 'I don't have enough,' 'I'm not ready,' or 'Who am I to start this?' When you don't see yourself as "qualified" or feel that you lack resources, the first step becomes the hardest.

Signs of this storm:

- Feeling Underqualified:

  Believing that you need formal education, years of experience, or perfect expertise before you can start.

  o Example: A skilled home cook hesitates to start a catering business because he does not have culinary school credentials.

- Feeling Under-Resourced:

  Focusing on what you don't have, things like money, connections, or tools, rather than identifying what you do have.

  o Example: A photographer thinks she cannot start a business because she lacks the latest camera equipment.

- Analysis Paralysis:

  Overthinking every step and becoming stuck in planning mode without ever acting.

  o Example: Someone with strong writing skills spends months researching 'how to start blogging?' but never writes a single post.

Many people also define 'resources' too narrowly, focusing only on tangible assets, such as money or professional qualifications.

However, your most valuable resources are often intangible and are already within your reach:

- Skills: Your natural talents, learned abilities, and hobbies (e.g., writing, designing, teaching, and organizing).

- Time: Even a few hours a day, when used intentionally, can lay the groundwork for something significant.

- Networks: Relationships with friends, family, or colleagues who can provide support, advice, or opportunities.

- Life Experience: Personal stories, challenges, and lessons you have learned that others can relate to and benefit from.

When you don't recognize these as valuable assets, you underestimate your potential for building your fishpond.

Solution:
Overcoming Initial Lack of Resources or Clarity:

Instead of focusing on what you don't have, start recognizing the potential in what you do have.

- Take Inventory of Your Resources:

   Start by identifying the skills, experiences, and tools you already have. Jot them down, no matter how small or unimportant they might appear. Ask yourself the same question you asked yourself in Chapter 6.

   o Example: A stay-at-home parent might list public speaking, organization, and planning as key skills she could monetize through event planning or coaching.

- Reframe Your Mindset:

   Concentrate on building something meaningful with the resources you already possess. Resources don't have to be perfect to be valuable. They need to be applied intentionally.

   o Example: You don't need to be an 'expert' to share your knowledge. Even teaching beginners what you know can be impactful.

- Start Small and Start Now:

  Clarity comes from acting, not from waiting for everything to be perfect. Instead of focusing on the entire fishpond, focus on building the first 'corner.'

  o Example: If you're a writer, start by publishing one short article this week.

- Find Strength in Your Story:

  Your struggles, failures, and lessons learned are among your greatest assets. Share them authentically to connect with your audience.

  o Example: Someone who overcame financial hardship could share budgeting tips through a blog or a workshop.

- Seek Support and Collaboration:

  Leverage your network to fill in gaps. Friends, mentors, or professional groups can provide ideas, feedback, or shared resources.

  o Example: Partner with a friend whose skills complement yours to build a shared vision.

ii. Problem:

Building Without Strategy:

When building your first fishpond, having a clear and actionable strategy is essential. Without it, your efforts may become fragmented, leaving you overwhelmed and yielding inconsistent or disappointing results.

Many people excited by the possibilities of building income streams or creative ecosystems fall into the trap of doing too much too fast. They may jump from one idea to the next, spreading their focus too thinly and failing to master any single endeavor. This scattered approach leads to inefficiency, incomplete systems, and a shallow, unstable fishpond.

- Example: A content creator might try to manage YouTube, Instagram, TikTok, and X (Twitter) simultaneously without a focused strategy for building and retaining an audience.

The lack of a precise plan results in burnout, inconsistent posting, and low engagement across all platforms. Instead of building momentum in one area, their energy is divided, and progress comes to a halt.

When you are unsure what you want to achieve, it is easy to fall into a cycle of reactive actions instead of intentional steps. Building without strategy often stems from:

- A Lack of Vision: Without knowing what you're trying to achieve, it's easy to get distracted by trends, short-term opportunities, or pressure to do everything at once.

- Chasing Trends: Jumping into the next 'hot' business idea without considering how it aligns with your skills or passions.

- Copying Others: Trying to replicate someone else's fishpond without understanding the strategy behind his success.

- Vague Goals: Setting goals like 'I want to make more money' without identifying specific steps to achieve that goal.

Solution:

Overcoming Building Without Strategy:

To avoid building without strategy, you must create a roadmap that prioritizes focus, direction, and clarity. Treat your fishpond like a well-planned project, one that is deliberate and adaptable.

You can do this by:

- Define Your Vision:

  Before you begin, clarify your 'why.' What is the goal of your fishpond? Is it financial freedom, creative expression, community impact, or personal fulfillment? A strong vision also allows you to filter out opportunities that don't align with your long-term goals.

- o Example: I want to build a sustainable income stream through my writing skills to support my family and inspire others.
- o Action Tip: Write your vision statement and keep it visible (e.g., on your desk or digital workspace) to remind you of your purpose as you build your fishpond.

- **Start Small and Focus on One Fish:**

   Don't try to do everything at once. Focus on building and perfecting one income stream, product, or system before expanding. Success in one area will create momentum, confidence, and resources to scale.

- o Example: A graphic designer starts with freelance client work, building a solid portfolio and reputation, before branching into selling design templates or teaching on platforms like Skillshare.
- o Action Tip: Identify one skill, resource, or opportunity you are most passionate about and begin building around it. Let it become your 'main fish' until it's thriving.

- **Set SMART Goals:**

   Outline specific, measurable, achievable, relevant, and time-bound goals to keep your efforts focused and aligned with your vision.

- o Example: Instead of "I want to sell more," set a goal like, "I will acquire five new clients within three months by networking and marketing my services."
- o Action Tip: Break larger goals into smaller, actionable steps. For instance, if your goal is to "create an online course," start with steps like outlining modules, recording lessons, and building a landing page.

- Prioritize and Sequence Your Efforts:

  When you have multiple ideas and opportunities, prioritize them based on feasibility, alignment with your skills, and potential impact. Instead of attempting to execute all your ideas at once, tackle one opportunity at a time, ensuring that each idea is stable before moving on to the next.

  o Example: If you want to create an online course and market it through a blog, focus on completing the course first. Once it's ready, shift your energy to content creation to promote it effectively.

  o Action Tip: Create a simple roadmap that outlines which opportunities you'll tackle first, second, and third. Stick to the sequence to maintain focus.

- Measure and Adapt:

  Regularly assess your progress to ensure you're on the right track. If something isn't working, analyze why and adapt your approach. A strong strategy is both intentional and flexible.

  o Example: If your freelance work isn't attracting enough clients, refine your portfolio, explore new platforms like LinkedIn or Fiverr, or adjust your pricing and marketing tactics.

  o Action Tip: Schedule monthly reviews to evaluate your progress; identify what's working and what's not, and adjust your goals or tactics as needed.

iii. Problem:

Fear of Failure:

Fear of failure is like a shadow that lingers on your path, whispering doubts and urging hesitation. It feels like standing on the edge of a high diving board, paralyzed by the endless 'what ifs.' What if the pond doesn't fill? What if the fish don't thrive? What if all my hard work leads to nothing?

These questions can feel overwhelming and stop you before you even begin. Yet, just as you cannot learn to swim without jumping into the water, you cannot build meaningful systems or lasting success without risking failure.

The fear of failure stems from two powerful sources: internal doubt and external pressures. Together, they form a mental storm that distorts our perception of challenges, risks, and setbacks.

- Internal Doubt:

  Fear magnifies obstacles, emphasizing what could go wrong, making challenges seem insurmountable while downplaying potential rewards, leaving you fixated on worst-case scenarios.

  o Example: An aspiring writer avoids publishing her work because she is terrified of criticism or rejection.

  Negative inner dialogue fuels this fear. The internal voice in your mind whispers, "You're not good enough." "You'll never make it," or "What's the point of trying?" This inner critic erodes confidence and keeps you frozen in a place.

  o Example: A person with a great business idea convinces himself it's not worth pursuing because he believes he'll never measure up to others in his field.

- External Pressures:

  Society often presents success as a straight, upward path, leaving little room for failure. Deviating from this perceived path can feel catastrophic.

  o Example: A recent graduate avoids pursuing her passion because her family expects her to follow a traditional, stable career.

  The thought of what others will think if you fail can weigh heavily on you. You may feel that one misstep will define you in the eyes of those around you.

o Example: A group of aspiring entrepreneurs hesitates to pitch their idea, fearing ridicule from friends or peers.

Remember, failure itself is often temporary, but the fear of failure can last a lifetime if it's left unchecked.

Solution:

Overcoming Fear of Failure:

The key to overcoming fear of failure is to reframe your perspective on it. Failure is not the opposite of success; it's part of it.

You can calm the storm by:

- Reframe Failure as a Stepping Stone:

  Failure isn't the end; it's another step in the journey. Every person who has built something worthwhile has faced setbacks and hasn't let those setbacks define them. Instead, they used them as opportunities to learn.

  o Action: Shift the question from asking, 'What if I fail?' to asking, 'What will I learn if I try?'

  o Example: An inventor doesn't see 99 failed prototypes as wasted effort but as 99 steps closer to the solution.

- Focus on the Process, Not Perfection:

  Waiting for the 'perfect' moment or outcome keeps you stuck. Success is about progress, not perfection. Growth comes from acting, even when it's messy or imperfect.

  o Action: Take small, intentional steps without obsessing over perfect results.

  o Example: A content creator uploads her first video, knowing it won't be perfect but treating it as a learning experience. Over time, each video improves, and she builds momentum.

- Treat Failure as Feedback:

  Failure is not a reflection of your worth. It's just feedback about your approach. When something doesn't work, analyze why, adapt, and try again.

  o Action: Ask Yourself:

    ▪ What went wrong?

    ▪ What can I do differently next time?

    ▪ What did I learn from this experience?

  o Example: An entrepreneur whose product launch fails uses customer feedback to tweak the offering and relaunch successfully.

- Build Confidence Through Small Risks:

  Confidence grows through action. Start with small, manageable risks to build momentum and resilience before tackling larger challenges.

  o Example: If public speaking terrifies you, start by practicing in front of friends or recording yourself on video. Gradually increase the audience size as you grow more comfortable.

- Learn from Others' Failures:

  Failure is a universal experience, even among the most successful individuals. By studying their journeys, you'll see that setbacks are often stepping stones to greatness.

  Examples of resilience:

  o J.K. Rowling: Rejected by 12 publishers before "Harry Potter" became a global phenomenon.

  o Steve Jobs: Was fired from his own company, Apple, before returning and leading it to unprecedented success.

- Focus on What You'll Miss by Not Trying:

  Instead of fixating on potential failure, think about the opportunities you'll lose if you never try.

  o Example: An artist finally shares her work with the world, realizing that staying hidden would have robbed her of the joy of connection and recognition.

The storm of fear can only win if you allow it to stop you. Take the first step, learn as you go, and trust in your ability to weather the challenges. Failure is not the end of the journey; it's often the very beginning of something extraordinary.

iv. Problem:

External Criticism and Doubt:

When building your fishpond, not everyone will see your vision clearly or appreciate the path you're forging. Friends, family members, and even society often project their fears, insecurities, or limited perspectives onto you.

While their intentions may be well-meaning, their doubts and skepticism can be discouraging, especially in the early stages, when the fruits of your labor are not yet visible.

External criticism and doubt are like storms that disrupt your focus and create unnecessary noise. These forces can sap your energy and plant seeds of self-doubt that threaten to derail your progress. If left unchecked, they can prevent you from fully realizing your vision.

- Well-Meaning but Misguided Advice:

  Friends or family members might question your decisions, not out of malice, but out of concern for your stability and security. Their advice often reflects their fears rather than the potential of your vision.

Example: A corporate employee who quits a stable job to start her own business may hear, 'Why would you leave a guaranteed paycheck?' or 'It's too risky. You'll regret it.'

- Comparison to Societal Standards:

  Society often defines success by traditional metrics, such as prestigious jobs, university degrees, or high salaries. If your journey doesn't fit into this framework, people may question its legitimacy.

  Example: Someone pursuing a career as a freelance writer or content creator might be compared to peers climbing the corporate ladder, with remarks like, "When will you get a 'real' job?"

- Skepticism in the Absence of Immediate Results:

  The early stages of any venture are often the most difficult. During this period, when progress is slow and results aren't visible, skepticism tends to surface. Critics might interpret the lack of instant success as failure.

  Example: A podcaster who spends months creating content without significant growth or income might hear, 'Why are you wasting so much time on this?'

- Self-Doubt Amplified by External Voices:

  Criticism from others can exacerbate your internal fears, creating a vicious cycle of self-doubt. Over time, you might begin to internalize the negativity and question your abilities.

  Example: An aspiring musician might think, "Maybe they're right. What if I'm not cut out for this?" and abandon his project prematurely.

Solution:
Overcoming External Criticism and Doubt:

You should know that you can't control what others think or say, but you can control how you respond to their criticism. The thing is to shield your vision from unnecessary negativity and stay focused on your path. Rise above external doubt and criticism.

- Clarify Your "Why":

  Your 'why' is the anchor that keeps you grounded during turbulent times. Knowing your purpose helps you stay committed, even when others doubt you.

  o Action Step: Write a personal mission statement that articulates your purpose. Keep it visible as a daily reminder of your bigger picture.

  o Example: "I am building this fishpond to create financial freedom for my family and live life on my terms."

  Whenever negativity threatens to distract you, return to your mission statement to remind yourself of the bigger picture.

- Focus on Progress, Not Approval:

  Instead of seeking approval, focus on measurable progress. Small wins, no matter how minor, are proof that you're moving in the right direction.

  o Action Step: Keep a journal documenting every milestone, skill learned, or positive feedback received.

  o Example: "I landed my first client today." or "This week, my blog traffic grew by 5%."

  These tangible markers of success will help drown out external negativity.

- Filter Constructive Feedback from Noise:

  Not all criticism is created equal. Learn to distinguish between constructive feedback that helps you grow and toxic negativity that only distracts you.

  o Action Step: Evaluate the source and intention of the feedback.

o   Constructive Advice: A mentor or expert offering advice to refine your work.

o   Toxic: A friend mocking your ambition with no helpful suggestions.

Accept advice from someone experienced in your field, but ignore baseless criticism from those unfamiliar with your journey.

- Surround Yourself with Supportive People:

The company you keep matters. Build a network of like-minded individuals who believe in your potential and encourage you through challenges. A positive community can counterbalance any negativity.

o   Action Step: Join online forums, mastermind groups, or networking events where people share ambitions like yours.

o   Example: An aspiring entrepreneur might join a Facebook group for small business owners to share ideas, gain encouragement, and learn from others' experiences.

- Let Results Speak for You:

Rather than arguing or trying to convince skeptics, focus on building your fishpond. Over time, your progress and achievements will silence doubters more effectively than words ever could.

o   Example: A freelance writer dismissed by critics can prove her worth by growing a portfolio of paying clients.

- Be Selective About Who You Share With:

Not everyone is meant to have a front-row seat on your journey. Share your plans and dreams with those who will offer constructive feedback or genuine encouragement.

- o Action Step: Identify a small circle of trusted individuals who can provide valuable insights and shield you from unhelpful negativity.

- o Example: Instead of sharing your startup idea with a skeptical relative, share it with a mentor who can guide and inspire you.

Always remember that those who criticize your efforts often don't see your vision because it's yours, not theirs. Trust your instincts, protect your progress, and let your results speak louder than the doubts.

v. **Problem:**

Resource Depletion or Financial Setbacks:

Just like a natural drought can shrink or dry up a thriving pond, financial setbacks can disrupt the growth and sustainability of your fishpond.

Whether it's an unexpected expense, a failed investment, or an economic downturn, these challenges can deplete your resources, leaving you feeling that progress is out of reach.

Financial setbacks are a reality every builder faces at some point. These 'droughts' come in many forms:

- Unexpected Expenses:

    Life often throws curveballs that drain resources, such as medical bills, emergency repairs, or sudden business costs. These unplanned expenses can disrupt your plans and force you to pause until you recover.

    - o Example: A freelance graphic designer's laptop breaks unexpectedly, halting work until he can afford a replacement.

- Poor Investments or Mismanagement:

    Not every investment pays off, and early missteps can lead to financial strain. Investing in tools, marketing, or products without proper planning or overspending on unnecessary upgrades can quickly deplete resources.

- o Example: A content creator purchases premium editing software but struggles to earn revenue in the early stages, creating financial stress.

- Overestimating Resources or Underestimating Costs:

Sometimes, the storm comes from within. Misjudging the amount of money, time, or effort required to sustain your fishpond can lead to mid-project setbacks.

- o Example: Someone writing a book overlooks the costs of editing, cover design, and marketing, consequently running out of funds before the project is complete.

- Revenue Droughts and Unpredictable Income Streams:

For many, income streams tied to freelancing, commissions, or seasonal demand can fluctuate wildly.

A slow month or an unexpected decline in revenue can feel like a drought that threatens the health of your pond.

- o Example: A social media influencer dependent on sponsorships experiences financial strain during periods when fewer brands are reaching out.

- Debt and Financial Obligations:

Debts, such as loans, credit card repayments, or outstanding financial obligations, can drain resources, making it difficult to reinvest in your fishpond. Instead of growing your pond, you may find yourself just staying afloat.

- o Example: A side hustler struggles to save money for business expenses while juggling monthly loan repayments.

Solution:

Overcome Financial Setbacks:

Financial challenges can feel overwhelming, but they can also be an opportunity to sharpen your strategy and find creative solutions. How to weather the storm of resource depletion:

- Start Small and Scale Gradually:

  Avoid overextending yourself financially in the early stages of your career. Focus on building manageable, low-cost systems first, and scale up as your resources and confidence grow.

  o Example: If you are starting a part-time tutoring business, use free space in your home, such as your garage, before investing in bigger space, paying rent, and needing transport.

  o Action Step: Break down your goals into smaller, affordable milestones to ensure sustainable progress.

- Create a Financial Safety Net:

  Set aside a portion of your income as an emergency fund to protect yourself during financial droughts. Start with small contributions and increase your savings over time.

  o Example: An online tutor can saves 10% of every payment, building a reserve for slower months.

  o Action Step: Automate savings to ensure consistency, even if it's a small amount, like 5-10% of each income stream.

- Minimize Unnecessary Expenses:

  Audit your spending and eliminate unnecessary costs to free up resources for growth. Prioritize needs over wants while stabilizing your fishpond.

  o Example: Cancel unused subscriptions, delay luxury purchases, and cut back on non-critical expenses.

    o   Action Step: Conduct a monthly financial audit to identify areas where you can save.

- Leverage Low-Cost or Free Resources:

Take advantage of free or affordable tools, platforms, and knowledge to keep costs down. Often, creativity and resourcefulness can offset a lack of capital.

    o   Example: Use free design tools like Canva, open-source software, or online courses to upskill without significant financial investment.

    o   Action Step: Research free trials or open-source alternatives before committing to paid tools or services.

- Monetize Your Existing Assets:

Look for creative ways to generate income using what you already have. Skills, tools, or even unused items can provide quick financial relief while you rebuild your fishpond.

    o   Example: A photographer rents out unused camera equipment or offers mini sessions to generate quick cash.

    o   Action Step: Take an inventory of your tangible and intangible assets to identify opportunities for immediate income.

- Seek Financial Guidance:

If managing finances feels overwhelming, consider seeking help from an expert or utilizing budgeting tools to enhance your financial system. A financial mentor or app can help you track your spending, set goals, and plan more effectively.

    o   Example: An entrepreneur struggling with cash flow issues seeks advice from a small business mentor and implements a better invoicing system.

  o Action Step: Research budgeting tools like Mint, YNAB (You Need a Budget), or QuickBooks to monitor expenses and plan smarter.

vi. Problem:
Difficulty in Scaling or Maintaining Balance:

Building a fishpond is an achievement, but expanding it, adding more 'fish' (new income streams), or taking on new responsibilities or opportunities is a delicate process.

Without proper oversight, rapid growth can lead to inefficiencies, burnout, or even the collapse of your ecosystem. Scaling isn't just about growing bigger but also about becoming smarter, thereby ensuring that your fishpond remains healthy and sustainable.

When growth happens too quickly or without proper structure, it can result in chaos rather than abundance. These challenges can be put into these categories:

- Over-Focusing on Growth at the Expense of Quality:

  Scaling often prioritizes quantity over quality, i.e., producing more content, taking on more clients, or expanding services to increase revenue. However, rapid growth without attention to quality can erode your reputation and damage trust with clients or audiences.

  o Example: A freelance graphic designer takes on too many projects to increase income, leading to missed deadlines and subpar work. Over time, this damages his professional image and client relationships.

- Loss of Balance Between Work, Life, and Well-Being:

  Scaling demands time, energy, and focus, which can tip your personal life out of balance. Pushing too hard can lead to exhaustion, strained relationships, and health problems, leaving you too depleted to sustain long-term growth.

o Example: A side hustler juggling multiple income streams and a full-time job sacrifices sleep and personal time, leading to burnout that disrupts both her personal and professional life.

- Overlooking Maintenance While Expanding:

Like a real fishpond, your existing systems require regular care and maintenance. When you chase new opportunities without sustaining what you've already built, your original success may deteriorate.

o Example: A blogger diversifies into podcasting but neglects his blog audience, resulting in a decline in traffic and ad revenue from his original platform.

Solution:
Strategies for Sustainable Scaling:

Scaling successfully is not about doing everything at once. It's about growing intentionally, balancing ambition with structure, and maintaining the quality and health of your ecosystem.

These are practical strategies to ensure sustainable growth:

- Perfect Before You Expand:

Before scaling, ensure that your current systems are optimized, stable, and efficient. Growth without a strong foundation can magnify inefficiencies and lead to instability.

o Action Step: Audit your current income streams to identify areas for improvement. Ask yourself:

▪ Are my current processes efficient?

▪ Is my customer experience consistent and of high quality?

▪ Are there gaps I can fill before expanding?

- o Example: A freelance writer refines her client's onboarding process and ensures the timely delivery of projects before taking on additional clients or launching a course.

- Grow Gradually and Test the Waters:

  Scaling too quickly can overwhelm you and your systems. Start small by testing new ideas, products, or services. Once you've confirmed your work, scale them strategically.

  - o Action Step: Introduce one "fish" at a time and evaluate its performance before expanding further.

  - o Example: A craft maker adds one product to her Etsy shop, testing its popularity before expanding her catalog.

- Build Systems That Scale With You:

  Invest time in creating processes, tools, or automations that enable your fishpond to grow without introducing chaos. Scalable systems, such as automated workflows, templates, or standard operating procedures, ensure consistency and save time as your responsibilities increase.

  - o Action Step: Use tools like project management software, email marketing platforms, or scheduling tools to automate repetitive tasks.

  - o Example: An online course creator uses an email automation system to handle student inquiries, hence freeing time for content creation.

- Delegate and Collaborate:

  Recognize when you've reached your capacity and need support. Delegating tasks to team members, contractors, or virtual assistants allows you to focus on high-value activities. Collaboration with others can also amplify your growth while reducing your workload.

o Action Step: Identify tasks that can be outsourced, such as bookkeeping, administrative work, or customer support. Consider collaborating with peers to share responsibilities.

o Example: A small business owner hires a part-time virtual assistant to handle emails and social media scheduling, freeing up time to focus on product development.

- Maintain a Work-Life Balance:

A healthy fishpond depends on the health of its builder. Scaling can be exciting, but it can also be exhausting if you neglect your well-being. Protect your energy by scheduling regular breaks, personal time, and moments of rest.

o Action Step: Block out time on your calendar for self-care, hobbies, and family. Treat these commitments as non-negotiable.

o Example: An entrepreneur sets aside Sundays as a no-work day to spend time with God and family, recharge, and avoid burnout.

vii. Problem:

The Scarcity Mindset:

The scarcity mindset is the belief that resources, success, and opportunities are limited in supply. If someone gains, it must mean that you lose. This perspective can breed fear, distrust, and hesitation, holding you back from collaborating, mentoring, or creating opportunities that benefit both you and others. Instead of viewing others as allies, they are seen as competitors, and success becomes a race rather than a shared journey.

This mindset not only limits your growth but also isolates you from the collective power of communities, networks, and partnerships. It builds unseen walls that prevent you from unlocking your full potential. Here are a few ways this mindset might hinder your success:

- Reluctance to Share Knowledge:

  The fear that teaching or mentoring others will lead to them surpassing you or taking advantage of you can make you withhold valuable insights. Ironically, this stops you from positioning yourself as an expert or thought leader.

  o Example: A graphic designer refuses to teach design techniques to budding creators, fearing that she'll lose clients. By not sharing, she misses opportunities to grow a loyal following, create an online course, or establish herself as a respected figure in her industry.

- Hesitation to Share Resources:

  Resources like tools, networks, or ideas can feel like precious assets. You may worry that sharing them will diminish their value or give someone else an advantage.

  o Example: A videographer refuses to recommend their favorite editing software to peers, fearing that they'll lose their competitive edge.

- Fear of Collaboration:

  The scarcity mindset views collaboration as a threat to individual success. In reality, collaborating with others often yields win-win scenarios that result in a greater impact and reach.

  o Example: A content creator avoids collaborating with others in his niche, fearing competition. As a result, he limits his exposure to new audiences and growth opportunities.

- Avoiding Mentorship or Helping Others:

  You may avoid mentoring or coaching others due to the fear that they will surpass you, thereby diminishing your own perceived achievements.

However, withholding guidance can limit your opportunities for growth, influence, and deeper connections.

- o   Example: A successful entrepreneur may hesitate to coach newcomers, believing that they might become competitors. In doing so, she misses out on the satisfaction and influence that come with shaping the next generation of innovators.

- **Isolation and Distrust:**

  This mindset leads to seeing everyone as a competitor, which isolates you and stunts your ability to learn from others. Over time, it closes doors to opportunities that could have arisen from collaboration and mutual support.

  - o   Example: An artist hoards commission opportunities, refusing to refer others, but ends up losing referrals and partnerships due to his lack of generosity.

Solution:
Overcoming Scarcity Mindset:

The key to overcoming the scarcity mindset is to adopt an abundance mindset, which is the belief that resources, success, and opportunities are not finite. By sharing, collaborating, and lifting others, you don't lose. Instead, you multiply. Adopting this mindset transforms relationships and unlocks greater opportunities for growth, creativity, and success.

Transition from a scarcity mindset to one of abundance:

- **Recognize That Success Is Not a Zero-Sum Game:**

  Another person's success does not diminish your own. When you help others grow, you expand your influence, strengthen your network, and create more opportunities for everyone.

  - o   Action Step: Celebrate others' successes rather than comparing them to your own. Use their wins as inspiration for what is possible.

- o Example: An independent author who shares tutorials and provides online tips on independent publishing builds a loyal following and attracts clients who trust his expertise. Sharing knowledge amplifies his authority in the field.

- Focus on Collaboration Over Competition:

  Instead of competing with others, seek opportunities to collaborate and create mutually beneficial outcomes. Collaboration often yields results that are far greater than those achieved by working alone.

  - o Action Step: Partner with someone in your field on a joint project, event, or campaign.
  - o Example: A fitness coach and nutritionist could team up to offer a comprehensive wellness program.

- Teach and Mentor Others:

  Teaching others reinforces your knowledge while positioning you as a leader. It creates trust, expands your network, and often leads to unexpected opportunities.

  - o Action Step: Start mentoring someone in your field or offering workshops and courses.
  - o Example: A freelance salesman could create a workshop teaching beginners how to pitch clients.

- Leverage Your Network Generously:

  Your network is one of your most valuable resources, and using it to connect others creates goodwill and strengthens relationships. Introducing people, sharing opportunities, or making referrals benefits everyone involved.

  - o Action Step: Refer a project or opportunity to someone else if you're too busy to take it on.

o Example: A graphic designer refers small projects to up-and-coming designers in her circle, building goodwill and opening the door for future collaborations.

- Celebrate Others' Success:

  Rather than seeing others' wins as a threat, use them as inspiration. Their achievements show what's possible and serve as motivation for your growth.

  o Action Step: Publicly acknowledge and uplift others' successes on social media or within your community.

  o Example: If a colleague lands a big client, share her win with a congratulatory post on social media.

The Unfinished Puzzle

Challenges are like the scattered pieces of a grand puzzle, some vibrant with potential, others appearing dark and seemingly out of place. At first glance, these pieces might seem chaotic and disconnected, each one a frustrating mystery. You need to sift through them, running your fingers over their uneven surfaces, searching for connections. It's frustrating work, especially when a piece that seems perfect refuses to fit where you want it to go.

Imagine standing before a table, the sunlight streaming through a nearby window, casting long shadows over the jumble of pieces. You find the edges first, straight lines and clean corners that snap together with satisfying precision. These are the easy decisions, the moments when life feels intuitive. But as you venture deeper into the pile, the work grows harder. The pieces that form the vivid heart of the puzzle are elusive, requiring you to slow down, squint at subtle patterns, and sometimes step back to see the bigger picture.

Progress is never linear. There are moments when every piece you try seems wrong. Frustration creeps in, tightening your chest and making you want to sweep the whole mess into a box and walk away, but then, almost by accident, a single piece falls into place.

It feels small, insignificant even, but it opens the door to the next piece, and then the next. With every connection, the chaos starts to make sense.

Building your fishpond works the same way. When faced with challenges, it's not about obsessing over a single 'wrong' moment but zooming out to see how it might connect to the bigger picture. That failure that stung you last week might teach you resilience tomorrow. The closed door might nudge you toward a better path. Like the pieces of the puzzle, every experience, no matter how frustrating or seemingly useless, has a purpose.

Lessons from the Puzzle:

i   Perspective Matters:

When a piece doesn't fit, it's not always about forcing it. Sometimes, you need to step back and look at the whole puzzle from a new angle. When building your fishpond, consider seeking advice, taking a break, or reevaluating your strategy.

Example: A student struggling with a problematic subject may benefit from shifting his study habits, asking for help from a tutor, or finding new resources to tackle the problem.

ii   Patience is Key:

Challenges require time and effort. The solution may not be immediately apparent, but persistence ensures progress. Each piece placed is a step closer to completion, no matter how slow the process feels.

Example: An entrepreneur launching a startup may face months of slow growth and countless rejections before finding his footing.

iii   Every Piece Matters:

Even the pieces that seem insignificant or frustrating at first eventually contribute to the larger whole. Even the struggles and mistakes play a role in completing the picture. What feels like failure today might be the critical piece you need tomorrow.

Example: A musician who struggles to learn a complex chord may find that mastery of that one piece opens the door to creating an entire song.

iv Celebrate the Small Wins:

Each piece placed correctly is a victory. When building your fishpond, every challenge you overcome, no matter how small, is worth celebrating because it moves you closer to the whole picture.

Example: A writer completing one chapter of a novel might celebrate this milestone, knowing it's a step closer to finishing the book.

When the final piece of the puzzle is placed, the once-chaotic array transforms into a cohesive, beautiful picture. What was once confusing and frustrating now makes perfect sense. In hindsight, every struggle, misstep, and frustration becomes part of the masterpiece. Without the darker pieces, the picture would lack depth. Without the vibrant ones, it would lack joy.

The Masterpiece of Your Fishpond

Think of each piece of your puzzle as a chapter in your story. Some chapters are easy to write, while others test your strength and creativity. Challenges are essential to your story. They are not distractions or inconveniences; they are integral to the growth process.

Like the joy of completing a puzzle, the fulfillment of achieving your goals lies not only in the result but in the process itself. The discovery, the effort, and the persistence are what make the journey meaningful.

The edges reflect your foundation, the basic skills, habits, and values that guide you. The vibrant pieces represent your passions and achievements. The darker pieces, though challenging, bring depth and perspective. Together, they form a complete, unique, and beautiful picture that tells your story—the masterpiece of your life.

As you step back to reflect on the puzzle, remember that its beauty comes from both its complexity and imperfection. Each piece, no matter how insignificant it once seemed, contributes to the whole. The struggles, triumphs, and in-between moments combine to tell a story of resilience, growth, and purpose. Your fishpond is not just a reflection of where you've been but also a testament to who you've become and the legacy you are building.

The meaning of life is to find your gift. The purpose of life is to give it away.

Pablo Picasso

Chapter 8

Sharing the Harvest

Imagine a vibrant fishpond, its surface shimmering under the golden sun, fish darting through the cool, clear water, their movements rippling outward to touch the grassy banks that cradle the pond.

The gentle splash of fish breaking the surface blends with the rustle of reeds swaying in the breeze. Nearby, the soil, dark and moist, brims with life, nourished by the overflow from the pond. This fishpond isn't just a source of sustenance but a lifeline for everything it touches.

Like a well-tended fishpond that feeds not just the land but an entire community, success becomes most meaningful when it is shared. Sharing the harvest isn't merely an act of generosity; it's a transformative process that amplifies the value of what you've created. When you share your wealth, knowledge, and resources, you turn individual success into collective progress.

Success isn't solitary. It's communal. It's also about what you can give, not just what you take. The accurate measure of achievement lies in its ripple effect: how your efforts impact others and inspire them to create their own success stories. Whether it's mentoring a colleague, sharing resources, or offering encouragement, it can spark growth in unexpected places.

A struggling local farmer, overwhelmed by a poor harvest, can receive help from a neighboring farm in the form of seeds to plant, advice on improving the soil, or even a helping hand to till the fields. With that assistance, the farmer can then rebuild and thrive. Later, when their harvest is plentiful, they can share their surplus with others—and so the cycle continues.

The Beauty of Abundance

Abundance, in its most valid form, isn't about hoarding. It's about flowing outward, touching lives in ways that create a ripple effect of growth. The knowledge you've acquired, the wealth you've built, or the opportunities you've unearthed all reach their fullest potential when they extend beyond personal gain. Generosity amplifies your impact, ensuring that the systems you build thrive far beyond your lifetime.

A mindset of scarcity, by contrast, clings tightly to resources, fearing loss or depletion. It hoards, restricts, and isolates. However, hoarding abundance is like building a dam that blocks the natural flow of water. Over time, stagnation sets in, and what was once a source of life becomes lifeless.

Abundance understands that resources are meant to flow. When abundance flows, it creates ecosystems of growth.

- Wealth flows outward to support causes, fund innovations, and uplift communities.

- Knowledge flows outward to educate, inspire, and empower.

- Opportunities flow outward to create new possibilities for others.

The fishpond doesn't run dry because it gives benefits. The fishpond thrives because its waters are in motion. The more it shares, the more it generates. A single act of generosity can spark a chain reaction, creating ripples that extend far beyond the initial contribution.

What will you share today? Perhaps it's a skill you've honed, passed on to someone eager to learn. Maybe it's a financial contribution that funds a dream or a word of encouragement that turns someone's day around.

The Seeds of Generosity

The fishpond is only the beginning. Its shimmering waters may feed the land, but its true magic lies in the seeds it nurtures, seeds that grow into new ecosystems of abundance. These seeds might take the form of ideas, resources, or skills shared with others, empowering them to build fishponds of their own.

Imagine your fishpond nourishing another, and then another, creating a vast network of interconnected ecosystems. Each new pond thrives on shared resources, mutual growth, and collective success. By planting these seeds, you turn your abundance into a ripple effect, spreading opportunity and transformation.

Abundance, at its core, isn't about just having enough; it's about having enough to give, and the more you give, the more connected you become to a greater network of shared growth and mutual upliftment. Like seeds scattered on fertile ground, your generosity plants hope and opportunity in places you may never see but where others will thrive. Let your fishpond inspire others, creating a forest of abundance where everyone can grow.

The Power of Shared Success

Success isn't meant to be hoarded. Kept to yourself, it's like a lone tree in an empty field, providing shade for a time but leaving the surrounding land barren. Shared success, on the other hand, is like a forest. Each tree nurtures the soil, shelters new growth, and creates an ecosystem where life flourishes.

The accurate measure of success is how it inspires and uplifts others. Whether it's passing on your knowledge, using your resources to address systemic challenges, or simply encouraging someone in their journey, sharing transforms personal achievement into collective progress.

i   Mentorship Multiplies Impact:

Mentorship is one of the most powerful ways to share your success. Teaching others to build their fishpond doesn't diminish yours; it expands your impact. When you mentor someone, you're not just passing on knowledge; you're planting seeds of confidence, opportunity, and independence in them.

Through mentorship, your influence extends beyond your achievements. The people you help create new opportunities for themselves, and, in turn, they inspire others. The ripple effect of mentorship is exponential, building new leaders, creators, and game changers.

ii Philanthropy Builds Purpose:

Wealth gains its most significant meaning when it's reinvested in solving problems, creating opportunities, and making the world a better place. Philanthropy transforms the fruits of your labor into tools for change, addressing society's most pressing challenges and creating lasting systems of abundance for others.

Consider the work of the Bill and Melinda Gates Foundation: By reinvesting their extraordinary wealth in global health, education, and poverty alleviation, they've turned personal success into a lasting legacy of impact. From funding vaccines that save millions of lives to providing resources for underfunded schools, their efforts prove that shared success has the power to create ripples of hope that reach around the world. Their focus on solving systemic problems transformed their achievements into a legacy that impacts millions of lives.

Philanthropy transforms material wealth into a force for good:

- Funding education to create a generation of empowered thinkers and doers.

- Addressing systemic issues like healthcare inequality, climate change, or poverty.

- Building sustainable opportunities that help communities thrive.

You don't need vast wealth to start giving back. Small acts of generosity, such as setting up a scholarship, funding a local initiative, or supporting a cause close to your heart, can create powerful ripples. These gestures not only help others but also deepen your sense of purpose and fulfillment.

iii   From Success to Significance:

Accolades or bank accounts don't measure true success. It's measured by the value you create for others. A solitary achievement might shine brightly for a moment, but shared success builds legacies. It can transform a solitary tree into a flourishing forest, an ecosystem where others can grow and thrive.

In today's competitive world, it's easy to fall into the trap of hoarding success. Society often celebrates the 'winners' who are the fastest, the strongest, and the ones who cross the finish line first. But true success isn't measured by what you've achieved alone. It's measured by the value your fishpond creates for others and the number of people you help gain independence.

Whether mentoring someone who stands where you once stood, funding initiatives that align with your values, or simply offering encouragement, or turning personal achievement into collective progress, such actions transform success into significance.

Think of the seeds you hold today: the skills you've honed, the resources you've built, and the knowledge you've gained. How will you plant them? Perhaps by guiding a struggling colleague, funding a scholarship, or simply being a source of encouragement.

The question is not whether you'll succeed but how many ecosystems your fishpond will inspire. So, what seeds will you plant today?

This Race Called Life

In a world driven by competition, it's easy to focus solely on winning, crossing the finish line first, but what if the race of life isn't just about how fast you run? What if the true purpose lies in who you bring along with you?

This brings to mind a story about a boy who once believed that winning alone was all that mattered, until he learned the true meaning of victory.

Once upon a time, there was a young boy who lived for running and racing. He thrived on the thrill of competition, the rush of adrenaline, and, most of all, the applause of the villagers who cheered him on. Every time he crossed the finish line faster than anyone else, his heart swelled with pride. Winning became his purpose, the applause his reward.

One day, the boy was challenged by two unlikely competitors: an elderly, frail woman and a blind man. He was confident in his speed and certain of his victory. The race began, and as expected, he sprinted ahead, leaving them far behind. When he crossed the finish line, he turned to the crowd, expecting their usual cheers and admiration. But this time, the crowd was silent.

Confused and hurt, the boy approached the village elder and asked, "Why are they not cheering for me? I won!"

The elder, with a kind smile, said, "Race them again, but this time, take their hands and cross the finish line together."

The boy was puzzled but agreed. In this second race, he slowed down. He walked beside the blind man, guiding him carefully, and supported the old woman as they moved together, step-by-step, toward the finish line.

When they crossed the line together, the crowd erupted with the loudest applause the boy had ever heard.

Bewildered, he turned to the elder and asked, "Why are they cheering now? I wasn't the fastest this time."

The elder replied, "In the first race, you ran for yourself. In this race, you ran for others. True success isn't about how far or fast you go, but it's also about who you bring along with you."

The boy stood still, letting the elder's words sink in. For the first time, he understood that a race wasn't just about speed. It was about the journey, about the people who ran it with him, and about the strength it took to help others cross the finish line.

This story beautifully illustrates the deeper meaning of success and how it becomes richer and more impactful when shared with others. It teaches us that individual achievement is hollow when it excludes others, while shared success brings lasting joy and fulfillment. As the elder wisely pointed out, "Winning for others is the true victory."

Let's break down the lessons from this tale:

i Success Is Meaningful When It Elevates Others:

In the first race, the boy achieved personal glory but left others behind. Even though he reached the finish line first, his triumph was empty because it lacked connection, empathy, and shared purpose.

In the second race, the boy discovered that true success is more than personal glory. It's about helping others succeed, guiding them when they stumble, and lifting them when they struggle. The joy of shared achievement far outweighs the fleeting satisfaction of individual wins.

True success is about lifting others, not just standing alone on the podium.

ii Collaboration Amplifies Victory:

While individual achievements are admirable, collective success is transformational. Helping others cross the finish line, whether in work, life, or relationships, can create a lasting legacy. Collaboration is more than just about the destination but about the bonds you build along the way.

Picture the boy holding the hands of the old woman and the blind man. Each step they took together built trust and connection. The journey was slower, but the shared victory brought deeper satisfaction. In life, the same is true: when we work together, the bonds we build are as important as the destination we reach.

iii   Redefining Winning:

The story challenges the traditional idea of winning as "coming first." Winning doesn't always mean standing in front of others. It can mean standing beside them, lifting them, and celebrating together.

Success is no longer just about how far or fast you can go. It's about how many people you bring along with you. It's about turning competition into collaboration and redefining winning as creating opportunities for others to succeed.

Just like the boy in the story, our most significant victories aren't measured merely by the applause we receive but by the lives we impact. The greatest harvest from your fishpond isn't what you take for yourself but what you share to uplift others.

How many people are you helping to cross the finish line? Are you building a fishpond that ensures that everyone around you can benefit from the harvest?

Because in this race called life, the finish line is never the end. It's a place where we can look back and see how far we've come together.

How to Share Your Success?

Sharing your harvest meaningfully starts with reflection. To give effectively, you must first understand what you have to offer and how it can impact others.

i   Define Your Harvest:

What are the fruits of your labor? Is it your wealth, knowledge, connections, or skills? Success takes many forms, and recognizing what you must share is the first step toward making a meaningful difference by seeing how your harvest can meet the needs of others.

ii   Define Ways to Share Your Harvest:

How can you share them? Align your harvest with the needs of others.

Think of your fishpond, overflowing, creating a river, feeding fields, filling reservoirs, and sustaining life along its path. The wealth, knowledge, and opportunities you share don't just meet immediate needs; they build pathways for growth, empowering others to create their fishponds. In doing so, you set off a ripple effect of abundance, transforming individual success into collective progress.

Cultural and Social Impact

When you share your harvest, you strengthen the cultural and social fabric of society.

i   Resilient Communities:

Shared resources create communities that are better equipped to face challenges. When people support one another, the entire group becomes stronger economically, socially, and emotionally.

ii   Building Connection:

Acts of generosity build strong, lasting bonds. They inspire goodwill, trust, and a deep sense of belonging.

iii   A Culture of Giving:

Many societies thrive on shared abundance. Sharing your harvest contributes to a culture of giving that transcends generations, creating a legacy of collective upliftment.

When your harvest becomes a source of strength for your community, you don't just change individual lives, but you also contribute to a stronger, more interconnected world.

Sharing as Leadership

Sharing your harvest positions you as a leader and a role model.

i   Inspiring Others:

Your actions demonstrate the power of generosity, encouraging others to give back in their own ways.

ii   Cultivating Future Leaders:

Mentoring and supporting others nurture a new generation of leaders who will continue to share and sustain this cycle of growth.

iii   Leading with Values:

Sharing reflects your commitment to values like compassion, equity, and sustainability. It establishes you as a leader who prioritizes impact over personal gain, showing that true leadership is grounded in service to others.

Generosity is leadership in action. It's a form of leadership that inspires, uplifts, and transforms those around you.

The Power of Shared Abundance

Generosity not only transforms lives but also transforms the systems within which we live. Here's how:

i   The Flow of Opportunity:

The more you share, the more opportunities flow back to you. Collaboration replaces competition, creating systems where everyone thrives.

ii   Breaking the Myth of Limits:

Sharing challenges the belief that success is finite. It proves that success grows when distributed, creating abundance for all.

The Ethics of Sharing

Sharing your harvest is not just an act of kindness; it is also a moral responsibility.

i   Giving Back to Society:

If your success has benefited from societal systems, networks, or opportunities, sharing ensures that you contribute back to the collective good.

ii Bridging Gaps:

Generosity helps close gaps in opportunity, providing others with the tools and resources they need to succeed.

iii Acknowledging Privilege:

Sharing is also a way of acknowledging the privileges that may have contributed to your success and working toward creating a more equitable playing field for others.

Generosity is a way to honor the interconnected systems that made your success possible. It ensures that the benefits of your journey extend beyond you, building a more just and equitable world.

Your Legacy of Abundance

Sharing your harvest can transform your success into something greater than yourself. You create rivers of opportunity, ecosystems of growth, and legacies that endure. As you move forward, remember:

- What does your fishpond have to offer?
- How can you share your harvest in a way that uplifts others?
- What ripples will you leave behind?

Ultimately, your greatest victories will not be in crossing the finish line alone, but in the lives you touch and the communities you empower.

What you leave behind is not what is engraved in stone monuments, but what is woven into the lives of others.

Pericles

Chapter 9

Building a Legacy of Abundance

The Endless Ripple

Building a legacy is like planting a tree whose shade you may never sit under. It's the culmination of your effort, creativity, and resilience, the mark you leave on the world. A true legacy isn't measured by accolades or personal achievements but by the lives you've touched, the opportunities you've created, and the systems you've built that flourish long after you're gone.

Imagine a gardener planting an orchard. He may not live to see the trees fully grown or taste the fruit at its sweetest, but he planted the trees anyway. Why? Because he knows that his work will sustain future generations.

In the same way, creating a legacy of abundance means planting seeds that others will benefit from, seeds that grow into ecosystems of growth, prosperity, and hope. Your fishpond, once a source of sustenance for you alone, can be transformed into a thriving ecosystem that feeds and inspires others.

Its overflow creates streams, nourishing fields and spawning new fishponds along the way. This is the essence of legacy: creating something that thrives beyond your presence and empowers others to build their success.

The Bridge Builder

Will Allen Dromgoole's timeless poem, The Bridge Builder, offers a profound metaphor for the essence of leaving behind a legacy of abundance. In the poem, an old man emerges from the shadows of a dense forest, his boots heavy with mud from the treacherous journey he has taken.

The river he's crossed roars behind him, its waters frothing and swift, but his eyes are already scanning the horizon. With the sun dipping low and painting the sky in hues of amber and violet, he sets down his pack, takes up his tools, and begins the painstaking work of building a bridge across the river.

A curious young traveler, observing the old man's effort, is perplexed. He approaches and asks, "Why are you building this bridge? You've already crossed the river and will never pass this way again." The old man pauses his work, looks up, and replies with wisdom etched in his voice:

> "Good friend, in the path I have come," he said,
>
> "There followed after me to-day A youth whose feet must pass this way. This chasm that has been as naught to me
>
> To that fair-haired youth may a pitfall be;
>
> He, too, must cross in the twilight dim; Good friend, I am building this bridge for him!"[17]

The bridge builder's selflessness captures the essence of a true legacy: creating something that benefits others, even when it doesn't directly benefit you. His selflessness illustrates the profound impact of thinking beyond one's immediate needs and considering the welfare of those who would come after him. It's a reminder that the most meaningful contributions are often those made for the sake of others.

---

17.   The Bridge Builder, https://www.poetryfoundation.org/poems/52702/the-bridge-builder

The Mindset of Legacy Builders

Building a legacy of abundance requires shifting your perspective. Like the old man in the poem, legacy builders think beyond their immediate needs and focus on how their actions can create a lasting impact for others.

Think of civil rights leaders like Rosa Parks or Martin Luther King Jr., who fought tirelessly for equality despite knowing that they might not live to see the full fruits of their labor. Their efforts laid a foundation that future generations continue to build upon.

i.   Thinking Beyond Yourself:

A legacy begins with the willingness to look beyond your desires and consider how your actions will affect future generations. The bridge builder didn't build the bridge for himself; he built it to ensure a safer journey for those who would come after him. Similarly, your fishpond's success is not measured by what you take but by what you leave behind for others.

Think of a teacher who stays after school to help a struggling student understand math, knowing that this knowledge might open doors the student hasn't even dreamed of yet. Or a small-town baker who mentors a young apprentice, passing on not just recipes but a craft, a livelihood, and a future.

What can you do today that will make someone else's path easier tomorrow?

ii. Creating Systems That Last:

Your fishpond is not just about leaving behind material wealth. It's about creating systems, opportunities, and pathways that endure. Whether it's mentoring future leaders, founding a business that creates jobs, or contributing to a cause that inspires change, your legacy is rooted in what you build and how it continues to serve others long after you're gone.

Andrew Carnegie, one of the wealthiest men of his era, not only built a vast fortune but also left a lasting legacy by establishing public libraries, providing millions with access to knowledge and opportunities for self-improvement that endured well beyond his lifetime.

iii. Empowering Others:

The old man's bridge empowered travelers to cross the river safely, reducing the risk and challenges they would otherwise face. Similarly, your fishpond should be a legacy of abundance, empowering others to overcome their struggles and achieve their goals. Such empowerment can take many forms, from sharing knowledge to offering mentorship or providing the resources and opportunities others need to succeed. Empowerment is the cornerstone of any lasting legacy.

Think of a farmer who teaches his neighbors sustainable irrigation techniques or a musician who volunteers to teach kids in underserved neighborhoods. These small, consistent acts of sharing knowledge or resources have a profound impact on people in ways that no one can fully predict.

Ripples of a Legacy

The bridge built by the old man in The Bridge Builder doesn't serve just one traveler; it benefits countless others who will pass that way in the future. This illustrates a profound truth that a legacy is not a single act but a ripple effect that grows and multiplies over time. Every bridge you build, every opportunity you create, and every life you touch contributes to this ripple, shaping the journeys of those who come after you. Imagine this ripple in action. Parents who always inspire their child to dream big. That child may grow up to become a scientist who might discover life-saving treatments. Those treatments go on to save lives worldwide. The parents may never see the full impact of his work, but their actions set the ripple in motion.

What bridges are you building today? Perhaps it's the encouragement you offer to a friend in need, the advice you share with a mentee, or the knowledge you pass on to your children. How will these actions ripple outward to create safe passage for others tomorrow? The answers to these questions define your legacy.

The Infinite Game of Legacy

Building a legacy of abundance isn't about reaching a final destination or achieving a singular goal. It's about participating in an infinite game where the focus is on perpetuating growth, progress, and impact beyond your lifetime.

- The accurate measure of a legacy isn't what it accomplishes while you're alive, but how it continues to serve and inspire others long after you're gone.

- A legacy isn't a static monument to your achievements; it's a living, breathing system that adapts, evolves, and continues to create value for future generations.

- A legacy is carried forward by the people who've been inspired, empowered, and equipped by your efforts.

For example, think of Jane Addams, the founder of Hull House. She didn't just provide immediate aid to struggling families in her Chicago community; she created a movement that redefined social work and inspired countless others to continue her mission of helping those in need.

Her legacy didn't stop with her life; it continues in every community center, outreach program, and social worker dedicated to helping others. This infinite game is about setting things in motion: systems that endure, values that resonate, and stories that inspire.

The Bigger Picture

Look at the sun rising each day, casting its light across the Earth. It doesn't choose where to shine or whom to favor. Its brilliance touches all, offering warmth, energy, and life. The legacy of abundance is much the same.

It's about an unselfish brilliance that shines outward, illuminating paths for others, nurturing their growth, and enhancing a sense of hope and possibility. Your principles become a moral compass for others. When you prioritize kindness, integrity, and generosity, these values ripple outward, shaping the lives of those who look to you for guidance and inspiration.

Your story, your struggles, and your triumphs become a source of hope and motivation. By sharing your journey, you light the way for those navigating their challenges. Like the sun that rises without fail, your legacy can become a consistent source of inspiration and empowerment for others:

- What Values Will You Instill?

  Think about the principles you want others to remember and carry forward.

- What Systems Will You Leave?

  Identify the structures or initiatives that will sustain growth beyond your lifetime.

- What Paths Will You Illuminate?

  Reflect on how your story can inspire others to navigate their journeys with courage and hope.

The Journey Continues

Even as you step back from your fishpond, your impact remains. The people you've inspired carry your lessons forward, weaving their own stories into the fabric of your legacy. Each person you've mentored, encouraged, or uplifted becomes a steward of the abundance you created, amplifying its reach and meaning.

The fishpond becomes more than a singular source of sustenance. It transforms into a network of interconnected systems, sustaining countless lives. Your impact continues to ripple outward, shaping futures you may never witness but have deeply influenced.

Ultimately, your legacy is not defined by the size of the fishpond you build, but by the magnitude of the ripples it creates. So, as you build your fishpond, remember it's about the bridges you build, the lives you touch, and the light you cast on the path for others. What ripples will you leave behind? And how will your legacy of abundance shape the world for generations to come?

Every man must decide whether he will walk in
the light of creative altruism or in the darkness of
destructive selfishness.

Martin Luther King Jr.

Conclusion

As you turn the final pages of this book, take a moment to reflect on the journey you've embarked upon, a journey that began with questioning the conventional maps and moving away from traditional paths toward a more meaningful and sustainable path. Life, as we've explored together, is much like tending to a fishpond.

It demands care, intentional effort, and the courage to adapt. Along the way, storms will challenge your resolve, deserts will test your endurance, and crowded fishponds will push you to innovate. Yet, each challenge you face is an opportunity to deepen your roots, sharpen your skills, and discover new ways to thrive.

Building Your Legacy

Your efforts, when shared, spark growth far beyond yourself. By sharing your harvest, mentoring others, and investing in the success of those around you, your accomplishments transform into a lasting legacy.

Like a fishpond that sustains an entire ecosystem, your generosity ensures that the ripples of your actions touch lives you may never meet.

An Invitation to Act

This is not the end. It's the beginning of a new chapter, one that only you can write.

- What will your fishpond look like?

- What seeds will you plant, and what ripples will you create?

- What have you discovered about your potential, the systems you can build, and the legacy you want to leave behind?

Your answers to these questions will shape a future that reflects your values, vision, and purpose.

Let what you've learned guide you. Please share your knowledge generously, face challenges with courage, and celebrate the beauty of abundance in all its forms. The journey ahead may not always be easy, but it will be meaningful, fulfilling, and deeply impactful if you choose to give and grow.

A Closing Reflection

The story of your life is still being written. Every choice you make, every effort you undertake, adds to that narrative. Let it be a story worth sharing, a story of creativity, freedom, resilience, growth, and boundless abundance.

As you step forward, may you remember that life is not just about what you achieve but about the lives you touch and the bridges you build.

Your fishpond is more than a source of sustenance; it's a symbol of your generosity, vision, and ability to create ripples that extend far beyond yourself.

Thank you for allowing this book to be a part of your journey. May your fishponds overflow with abundance. May the storms you face strengthen you, and may the bridges you build inspire others to thrive.

May your efforts ripple outward, touching lives far beyond your own. May you find true fulfillment in the beauty of giving, the joy of growth, and the profound satisfaction of leaving the world better than you found it.

Go forward boldly and let your light shine.

Metaphor Glossary

1. **Abundance Mindset**
   A perspective that sees resources and opportunities as limitless and flowing freely, rather than scarce, growing when shared rather than diminished.

2. **Bird in a Cage**
   Feeling trapped in systems or environments (e.g., corporate structures) that stifle creativity, freedom, and potential.

3. **Borrowed Ladder**
   A career path or system designed by someone else, leading you toward goals that aren't your own.

4. **Bridge**
   A solution or system that connects challenges to opportunities, enabling growth and independence.

5. **Bridge Builder**
   A person who creates opportunities, systems, or pathways that benefit others, even without personal gain.

6. **Building Your Own Ladder**
   Designing a personal path to success that reflects your passions, values, and unique goals rather than conforming to societal expectations.

7. **Challenges as Storms**
   Obstacles and setbacks that feel destructive but provide the lessons, resilience, and growth needed for long-term success.

8. **Compass**
   A device that helps you find your true north: what truly matters to you—passions, values, long-term goals, and vision.

9. **Compass Mindset**

   The ability to use creativity, talents, and passion to design systems that solve problems, inspire change, and empower others.

10. **Conveyor Belt**

   The rigid, standardized approach of traditional education systems, focusing on conformity and predictability rather than individuality.

11. **Cooking Without a Recipe**

   Learning through experimentation, adaptation, and creativity rather than following rigid instructions.

12. **Creativity as a Spark in the Darkness**

   Creativity illuminates possibilities and offers hope in uncertain or challenging moments.

13. **Crowded Fishponds**

   Overly saturated industries or markets with limited opportunities and fierce competition.

14. **Desert of Scarce Fishponds**

   A harsh environment (e.g., oversaturated job markets) where opportunities are scarce, requiring resilience and resourcefulness to survive.

15. **Elephant Rope**

   Limiting beliefs instilled by societal norms or education systems that hold individuals back from achieving their full potential.

16. **Escalator to Nowhere**

   Career advancement within rigid systems (e.g., corporate ladders) that often leads to unfulfilling goals.

17. **Failing Forward**

   Turning mistakes into valuable lessons, using failure as a stepping stone for growth and improvement.

18. **Fish as Income Streams**

   Diverse sources of income or value generated from your work or systems that sustain independence.

19. **Fishing Hook**

A single academic qualification (e.g., certificate or degree) that represents specialized knowledge but doesn't guarantee success on its own.

20. **Fishing Net**

Multiple academic qualifications (e.g., multiple degrees or certifications), which may appear impressive but require practical application to be valuable.

21. **Fishing School**

Academic institutions (from elementary to university) that teach skills but often fail to provide practical systems for applying those skills.

22. **Fishpond**

A self-sustaining system of value that represents independence, creativity, and abundance in life or work.

23. **Fishpond Harvest**

The fruits of your labor—what your systems produce for yourself and others, including wealth, knowledge, and opportunities.

24. **Fountain of Ideas**

Creativity as an endless, self-replenishing source of innovation and inspiration, where each idea feeds the next.

25. **Garden of Ideas**

A diverse and dynamic environment that supports the growth of creativity, individuality, and adaptability.

26. **Gap**

A problem or challenge that represents the distance between your current state and where you want to be.

27. **Golden Handcuffs**

High-paying or stable jobs that provide financial security but trap individuals in unfulfilling lifestyles or careers.

28. **Infinite Game of Legacy**

A focus on long-term progress, impact, and growth that outlives individual achievement.

29. Labyrinth of the Corporate Ladder

The complexity and frustrations of navigating rigid corporate systems that often fail to provide personal fulfillment.

30. Legacy That No Longer Fits

The outdated priorities and systems inherited from the past, which no longer align with modern needs or values.

31. Maze of Misaligned Goals

The pursuit of objectives that don't align with personal passions or values, leading to confusion and dissatisfaction.

32. Monoculture Farm

Vast field where every seed is meticulously planted with the expectation that it will grow into the same type of plant, look the same and serve the same purpose.

33. Mountains Beyond Mountains

The endless journey of growth, where each achievement reveals new challenges and opportunities.

34. Nest of Comfort Zones

A secure but limiting space that stifles growth and innovation if clung to for too long.

35. Overfishing the Pond

Unsustainable practices in work or life that exhaust a resource or system, leading to decline.

36. Open Sea

A life created on your own terms, guided by your passions, creativity, and unique vision.

37. Problem

The difference between your current state and your desired future state.

38. Puzzle

Life's challenges and obstacles, where each piece—including struggles—contributes to the larger picture of success.

39. **Rainbow After the Storm**

    The promise of growth, clarity, and reward that follows overcoming challenges and hardships.

40. **Seeds of Generosity**

    The potential for ideas, resources, or actions to grow and empower others when shared.

41. **Shiny Fishing Rods**

    Degrees, credentials, or tools that look impressive but don't guarantee success without the right environment or application.

42. **Stagnant Pond**

    A life or system lacking growth, motion, or change, leading to stagnation and decline.

43. **Storm as Teacher**

    The idea that challenges provide critical lessons and strengthen your foundation for future growth.

44. **System of Independence**

    A personal framework or "fishpond" that provides value, freedom, and self-sustainability, empowering you to thrive.

45. **Setting sail**

    Embarking on a journey of independence and purpose, designing systems that benefit yourself and others.

46. **Shore**

    Comfort zones that feel safe but limit exploration and growth.

47. **Societal Map**

    Traditional paths prescribed by society (e.g., study, work, retire) that don't always lead to fulfillment.

48. **The Builder's Toolbox**

    Practical skills and tools that align with your passions and help you overcome challenges and create systems of success.

49. **The Escalator to Nowhere**

    The monotony and futility of pursuing success without questioning its alignment with personal fulfillment.

50. **The Fishpond Race**

The idea that success isn't about being first but about bringing others along with you.

51. **The Garden of Creativity**

A thriving ecosystem that grows through consistent planting, nurturing, and harvesting of creative ideas.

52. **The Leap from the Nest**

Leaving the comfort zone of traditional systems (corporate jobs or dependency) is compared to a bird leaping from its nest into the sky.

53. **The Unfinished Puzzle**

Life as a work in progress, where every challenge or success adds to the bigger picture.

54. **Trained Fisher**

Educated individuals (e.g., graduates) equipped with knowledge but not always the tools to create opportunities.

55. **Tree of Legacy**

A sustainable system that provides inspiration, resources, and opportunities for future generations.

References

1. Aston Martin V2 Vanquish, https://www.007.com/the-vehicles/aston-martin-v12-vanquish/
2. Gillian Lynne, https://en.wikipedia.org/wiki/Gillian_Lynne
3. Malala Yousafzai, https://malala.org/malalas-story
4. Art & Fear: The ceramics class and quantity before quality, https://excellentjourney.net/2015/03/04/art-fear-the-ceramics-class-and-quantity-before-quality/
5. Richard Branson, https://en.wikipedia.org/wiki/Richard_Branson
6. Who is Larry Ellison, https://www.investopedia.com/terms/l/larry-ellison.asp
7. Finland's children-centric school system, https://www.humanium.org/en/finlands-children-centric-school-system-a-global-model-for-success/
8. Finnish Education System, https://www.edunation.co/blog/finnish-education-system-the-best-in-the-world/
9. The Apollo 13 Accident, https://nssdc.gsfc.nasa.gov/planetary/lunar/ap13acc.html
10. 10 School Dropouts Who Became Billionaires, https://businesselitesafrica.com/10-school-dropouts-who-became-billionaires/?v=a1555463c361
11. Stories Of 9 Indians Who Quit Stable Jobs To Pursue Their Passions, https://homegrown.co.in/homegrown-voices/stories-of-10-indians-who-quit-stable-jobs-to-pursue-their-passions
12. High Tech High Charter School, https://en.wikipedia.org/wiki/High_Tech_High_charter_schools
13. Jeff Bezos, https://en.wikipedia.org/wiki/Jeff_Bezos
14. Jack Ma, https://en.wikipedia.org/wiki/Jack_Ma

15. The Ideal Mindset: 31 Famous Individuals Who Overcame Huge Setbacks, https://www.becomedamngood.com/post/the-ideal-mindset-14-famous-individuals-who-overcame-huge-setbacks

16. The Industrial Age Roots of General Education, https://psu.pb.unizin.org/generaleducationfortheinformationsociety/chapter/the-industrial-age-roots-of-general-education/

17. I have not failed. I've just found 10,000 ways that won't work: https://www.naphill.org/tftd/thought_for_the_day_monday_march_20_2017/

18. Elon Musk, https://en.wikipedia.org/wiki/Elon_Musk

19. AirBnB, https://en.wikipedia.org/wiki/Airbnb

20. A story on how Apple Got the Idea of ' Slide to Unlock, 'https://www.linkedin.com/pulse/story-how-apple-got-idea-slide-unlock-parth-gohil

21. How Argentina legend Diego Maradona helped crown Barcelona star Lionel Messi as the free-kick king, https://www.dailymail.co.uk/sport/football/article-6986759/How-Diego-Maradona-helped-crown-Lionel-Messi-free-kick-king.html

22. Bill & Melinda Gates Foundation, https://en.wikipedia.org/wiki/Bill_%26_Melinda_Gates_Foundation

23. The Bridge Builder, https://www.poetryfoundation.org/poems/52702/the-bridge-builder

24. How a bakery went from creating bespoke cakes to delivering DIY kits during the COVID-19 pandemic, https://en-gb.facebook.com/business/news/how-a-bakery-responded-to-coronavirus

25. I have not Failed, https://www.naphill.org/tftd/thought_for_the_day_monday_march_20_2017/

26. Charles Darrow, https://en.wikipedia.org/wiki/Charles_Darrow

27. Carrot and stick, https://en.wikipedia.org/wiki/Carrot_and_stick

28. Jane Addams Hull House Museum, https://www.hullhousemuseum.org/about-jane-addams

www.ingramcontent.com/pod-product-compliance
Lightning Source LLC
Chambersburg PA
CBHW022039190326
41520CB00008B/651